A MOTHER'S STORY
OF CHANGING TIMES

The Pages of Life
A Memoir

Information & ordering:
Millie J. Chandler
5126 Morning Glory Lane
Loves Park, IL 61111
815.877.9053MilJChandler@aol.com

Cheap Trick CD Cover Art + Photos
© 2003 Cheap Trick Unlimited, Inc. 2003

Dedicated to Father & Sons

Clifford J. Chandler

James D. Chandler

Richard J. Chandler

Gregory A. Chandler

Introduction

Following forty-one years of marriage, a mother of three grown sons and five grandchildren was completing her life as a single woman…

Chandler tells her memoir through a series of subject matters. It is a way of turning the pages of her life personally and connecting it with all of our collective stories of changing times.

She began this journey as a little girl growing up during the trying years of the Great Depression of the 1930's. Then marriage, children, a series of careers, divorce, beginning college at age sixty-seven and now, the telling of her life story.

As the oldest student at both North Hennepin Community College in Brooklyn Park, MN where she graduated with an AA Degree and at Metropolitan State University in Minneapolis and St. Paul, Minnesota, where she received her BA Degree, Millie Chandler became a 'Story Teller.'

Chandler tells her memoirs through a series of subject matters, as a way of turning the pages of her life.

While attending North Hennepin Community College, she became a staff writer for the college paper as a journalism student and had numerous stories published. At Metropolitan State University in 1997, she took classes in journalism and memoir writing where she wrote stories each week. In 2001, after moving from Minnesota to Illinois, she became a free-lance writer for The Journal, a weekly local newspaper. This resulted in having over twelve human-interest stories published.

Contents

Part I - A Story That Inspired Me

Part II - Stories From The Time Of My Early Years

Part III - Stories From My Married Years

Part IV - My Sons

Part V - Separation & Divorce

Part VI - My New Life As A Single Person

Part I
A Story That Inspired Me

A significant part of my inspiration to write my own memoir was this short, life story told to me by Frances M. Miell, when she was eighty-four years of age. It begins from her birth and ends with her husband's death, filled with family values and the changing history in our country and world.

For me, The Frances M. Miell Story continues to inspire me. It has made a lasting impression in my life. Perhaps may in yours.

The Frances M. Miell Story

In many ways, Frances M. Miell's story is the story of America growing up. Family values are something that Miell learned at an early age and she lived by those values all of her life. They represent the ethos of the American character and spirit of the 20th Century.

On November 28, 1914, Miell was born on the Cass Lake Indian Reservation. Her father was the junior pharmacist on the reservation. He was born in Sweden and her mother was born in England. She was the baby of the family and had two older brothers, Ralph and Donald. At the time of her birth, The First World War was ongoing.

Austria-Hungary declared war on Serbia.

Germany declared war on Russia and France.
England declared war on Germany.
Later other nations became involved.
Woodrow Wilson was our President.

Miell said, "I was a home-delivered baby born on an Indian Reservation and with the help of a nurse, I was becoming an alcoholic." In those days, it was standard practice for a new mother had to have bed-rest for nine days. A nurse came in each evening to check on the mother and child. Each evening the baby was cranky and before the nurse left, she had quieted her for the evening. After the nine days, the nurse no longer came to the house. The cranky evenings returned. The father found a spoon by the wash-stand and after careful observation, he discovered the smell of whiskey on the spoon. He knew the nurse was giving their new child whiskey to quiet her to sleep each night. It took some time before the fussing stopped.

"There was no more whiskey for me," said Meill.

In March, President Wilson directed the arming of merchant ships and on April 6, 1917, a special Congressional-Session and the Declaration of War were signed, and that was the United States entry into World War I.

In 1917, the family moved to Backus, Minnesota. Her father bought the only drug store in town. The world was in a mess. Business was not good. No one seemed to have money to pay bills. People would come to the drug store to buy medicine, but did not have cash to pay. "My Dad would never turn any one away that needed medicine, so he put it on their accounts and most accounts were never paid," said Miell.

"One of my father's Indian customers became a special friend. He could not pay his bill so he brought him a beautiful hand-beaded pillow in payment. My dad gave me that pillow. I recently passed on the pillow to my grandson, Larry."

In 1922, the war was over and United States began to develop its World Peace policies. Miell was now age seven.

"I roller skated to school. First my dad would insist that I practice the piano each morning before school. He was very strict," she said. "Then I would join my friends waiting for me on our front porch. Off we went on our skates. It was so much fun."

"If we were early, we would all stop at a place the kids called 'By Crackie,' because the man that lived there would always say, 'By Crackie'. "We stopped there to play croquet," she recalls. "When we heard the first bell ring, we would run as fast as we could to make it to school on time so we would not be in trouble. One day we came late ending our stop at 'By Crackie'.""Except for that one time, I was never late to school and always had perfect attendance," she says. High values were instilled upon her.

Miell remembers when she played the piano for a funeral at a young age and her feet did not touch the pedals. She was scared because she did not know how it would sound and played and played until everyone left the church. "Then mother told me, you could stop playing now."

Her dad played the cornet until he no longer had his own teeth and later he played the violin, she played the piano, her brother, Ralph played the cornet and Donald drummed a wooden spoon on a breadbox. "Mother would sit back and smile when the family band assembled for the jam session." said Miell.

The stock market crash in October of 1929 marked the start of a severe depression. Economic conditions grew increasingly worse. Unemployment increased, banks and businesses failed and factories closed. No one seemed to have any money. "I didn't know we were poor.

Mom and Dad never complained. Mom made all our clothes. I never had anything store-bought until I was in Junior High School," Miell said.

"They bought me a coat and I was so proud of it. One day, my best friend, Buella's, boy friend, died and did not have a coat to wear to the funeral so I loaned her my new coat. I played the piano at that funeral."

When she was a senior in high school, she met her future husband, Richard, at a grocery store. He waited for her to graduate and on July 2, 1932, they were married and lived with her family.

"The next winter we moved to Hackensack, MN into a small cottage down by the lake. The house had no running water, radio, or refrigerator. We kept food in a hole lined with tarpaper to keep milk, cream and meat fresh. We had a two-holer outdoor toilet we called 'Joe- Bigaloo-Place'."

At that time, "Richard was working at a grocery store earning approximately $40 per month, and he would bring home 10 cents worth of hamburger, which was enough meat to prepare a meal. It cost $5 per month for rent, but $8 in the summer because it was more expensive to live by the lake in the summer. We put a crib in the corner of our bedroom for our son, Roger. We had a round wood stove in the living room, cut and chopped all our wood for heating and cooking. It was a happy time in our life," said Miell.

"When Roger was born, the closest hospital was

50 miles away in Brainerd, Minnesota and we did not have a car. A neighbor loaned us their Model-T to get me to the hospital. The snow was blowing and it was bitter cold without a heater in the car. I was freezing and scared to death." Later, her daughter, Carol-Ann, was born in the same hospital."

Our country was preparing for war. In 1940, Franklin D. Roosevelt was elected President for the third time.

That year, her husband, Richard and his father, bought some tax delinquent property in Hackensack, Minnesota, across the railroad track. Together, they built a new three-bedroom home. It had two bedrooms upstairs, bathroom downstairs, all large rooms, a full basement and garage. It took years to complete and they moved into their new home in 1941. They paid cash for every load of lumber. Richard worked as a clerk at the Post Office earning $100 per month.

In 1944, Richard was drafted into the U. S. Navy and went to the Great Lakes for his training, then was transferred to NYC Naval Base to serve at the Fleet Post Office. From there, he transferred to San Francisco Fleet Post Office for a two-year tour of duty.

In 1942, they had their first telephone installed. They decided that they could only afford to call each other once a month, limiting the time of their conversation to five minutes. Each of the children had one minute to talk with dad and Miell had the first and last minute and a half allotted to her. At the end of each call, everyone was crying.

"He was gone for Christmas." she said. "When Richard left for the Navy, I was unprepared for the separation and missed him very much. I spent a lot of time in tears and seemed to be just watching the trees grow. I was very lonely. We wrote to each other daily and I prize my wonderful letters Richard wrote and still have every one of them."

"I had two gardens to take care of. One was planted with potatoes and the other with corn. I received $30 as a dependent allotment each month from the Navy. It was never enough, so both our parents helped us with some of the finances and the food." Richard was discharged from the Navy in 1946 and returned to his job at our town's post office."

In 1982, they celebrated their 50th Wedding anniversary. Richard's health started failing. The last six years spent in Hackensack were not easy for them. Her husband showed many signs of his progressing Alzheimer's disease.

In 1992, Miell and her husband decided to move to Maranatha Place in Brooklyn Center, MN because it would be more convenient for everyone if they lived there. They liked the fact that the nursing home care center was joined to the apartment complex. It was an enormous responsibility to become the caregiver to her husband. She thought about it many times. "The least I could do is make him comfortable. If I were the one that was sick, Richard would be doing the same things for me. He was my life and I loved him very much."

Getting him in and out of bed and a chair as well as giving him a daily shower, were very challenging for her. After many showers for Richard with Miell getting all wet, a system was finally worked out. She decided to combine their showers saving time and her clothes no longer got wet. Another hurdle had been crossed.

Richard became easily upset. He was not only suffering from Alzheimer's, was diabetic, needing a special diet, which Miell prepared. He was also became confined to a wheel chair.

It was time for him to be moved to the care center. Each day, she came to the care center to visit and took Richard back to the apartment in his wheel chair to spend one hour together.

On July 2, 1992, Miell and her husband spent a quiet time celebrating their 60th Wedding Anniversary with children and grandchildren. They had seven grandchildren, six great grandchildren and another great grandchild expected.

On November 30, 1995, Richard died. "He knew me until two days before he died," she said.

Miell's life continued and she became terribly lonely. She was now a grieving widow and had to adjust to life without Richard. Her friends and family stood by her for moral support and would not allow her to shut herself away. She eventually 'got back into life' and became involved with others. I'll end her story with this poem. She said, "Attitude, I believe in it faithfully." She had this poem framed and hanging over her desk.

"Attitude"
By: Charles Swindoll

"The longer I live, the more I realize the impact of Attitude on Life.
Attitude, to me, is more important than facts. It is more important than the past, than education, than money, than circumstances, than failures, than successes, than what other people think or say, or do. It is more important than appearance, giftedness or skill. It will make or break a Company…A Church…A Home.

The remarkable thing is we have a choice every day regarding the attitude we will embrace for the day. We cannot change our past…We cannot change the fact that people will act in a certain way. We cannot change the inevitable.

The only thing we can do is play on the one string we have, and that is our attitude…I am convinced that Life is 10% what happens to me and 90% how I react to it. And so it is with you…We Are In Charge Of Our Attitude."

Part II
Stories From The Time Of My Early Years

For years I blamed my father for many things. In 1998, I took a history class on The Great Depression of the 1930's and finally learned the actual history of our country. That helped me learn that many of the reasons my family's life was difficult were not my father's fault. I wrote this troublesome story of growing up, which took nearly six months to write, and sent it to all my sisters and brothers. Today, I still have this belief firmly in my mind, "I never want to run out of food or money in my lifetime."

Yesterday's Memories Of My Father

Our country was in The Great Depression of the 1930's. Many people everywhere during this time were suffering from the hardships of trying 'to keep a roof over their families' head and something to eat on the table', and so was my father.

The year was 1932 and our home was located

on a hill at 75 Spring Street in the little town of Monticello, New York. The population was under 3,000 and located about 100 miles northwest of New York City. There were a few houses spaced far apart on our street.

Across from our house stood a huge dark green one with a great porch. Living there were two very rich elderly spinster-sisters, that we hardly every saw. My sisters and I would longingly look across at that house, wondering what it would be like to see the inside of that home. We knew our cold, old house, with the dirt-bottom cellar that opened by a trap door at the back of our house, was not equal to the one across the street.

It was morning time. At the head of our wood table sat my father…His big, fat, five-cent cigar was in his mouth, lit and burning. He was never without it. He was 5'10" tall, had a lean body with dark wavy hair. He looked to be a gentle, kind man with an expression of despair

Albert Hartman with cigar

always on his face. We were about to eat breakfast.

All six of us children sat at the table on old wooden hard chairs and we were each served lumpy oatmeal from an enamel bowl. We did not have milk or butter to put in the oatmeal and that is why it seemed to me to be lumpy. If we were lucky on a particular morning, we got a piece of bread too. After finishing breakfast, we left still hungry.

Our short, nice looking, but stingy mother never sat down. She was the one in charge of food. While cooking, the coal stove warmed a small portion of the house. Unless we stood close to the warm stove with our hands over the top, we were still freezing in the wintertime.

After breakfast, we often listened to the news on the one luxury item we owned, our radio. My father would then get ready to leave for the day. He always wore the same thing. His apparel included an off-white, half-pressed shirt with a yellowish color. His necktie was wide and ugly. His pants were extremely worn and ready for the trash, but they were his only pair. My father's suit jacket was not much better.

His high, black shoes were scoffed. When the leather in the soles wore so thin that they were wearing through, cardboard was cut and placed inside the bottom of the shoes so they could continue to be worn. I guess he had to remember not to walk on any pointed objects. An old felt worn hat completed his attire and off he would walk for the day. By today's standards, my father looked like a bum. During those times, he didn't seem to be dressed significantly better or worse than any of the men in our town.

He headed to the Candy and Cigar Store and hung around with other unemployed men in the back room, where mostly the men played cards and worried. My father did not play cards because he did not have the money. He just hung around for the day and worried. It was a good thing we were on relief, so we could at least eat and not starve.

My mother's job was to cook and keep us alive. She did a good job, too. Sometimes we had soup made from a meat bone, purchased for a cost of five cents. My mother would add anything she had in the kitchen to the bone soup. If we were lucky and the butcher felt generous, there was a little meat left on the bone. We had potatoes, bread and whatever the relief people from the Federal Government, periodically delivered to our home.

The milkman came to our house at night. There

were new laws passed regarding the sale of milk. It had to be pasteurized and bottled, to be sold legally. Our milkman was selling 'black-market' milk out of his big tin milking can, which was called 'raw-milk'. It cost a lot less. As long as no one knew found out, we could continue to buy it. Even so, we never had enough milk to drink when we were children.

My father would get a 'sign painting' job once in a while. He was a good sign painter and would paint sale signs for grocery stores, showing their current sales. He would set up two wooden saw-horses in our living room, placing a flat long board over the top and then cutting a long piece from his roll of paper for the size of sign needed. He used black and red paints. It seemed to me that he was a fast painter. After he completed a sign and letting it dry, he would roll it up and take it to town. Payment for such a sign was typi-cally $2.00.

I remember our home filled with odors. The oil paint and turpentine used for cleaning brushes, my father's cigars and at times, the smell of deli-cious meat-bone soup filled the air.

Before my father would leave for town, he would ask us girls to try to find any half-used coal that had been tossed away with the ashes from places that other people had dumped their burnt coal. We would take our pails and pick up one coal at a time, carefully looking to see if it still had a little bit of black remaining. This second hand coal would help warm our home that night.

The depression days were a terrible time for us children. We did not understand why we were poor and always hungry. My father was upset most of the time, while mother kept nagging about money, food and anything else she could. She often told our father, "The girls were naughty today, and I can't do anything about it. They will not listen to me and you have to punish them."

In the 'old days', punishment meant a spanking. Off would come my father's wide, black, heavy leather belt. He insisted that we take our pants down so we could feel the hard blows on our bare skin, and only then, would we remember not to be naughty. Those spankings hurt and left red belt marks on our bottoms. We were afraid of our father. This would be considered 'child abuse' today. The father was in charge and boss of his home and family. That was one lesson we knew.

It was now 1938 and the depression of the 1930s seemed to go on and on. We had to move from our house at 75 Spring Street. We were evicted. Too many months went by without rent payments from my father. He did not have any money. We had to move to a big, ugly, dark brown house in bad need of repair, located on 16 Oakley Avenue. It was a tall square house with two front porches. The one on the first floor was okay, but on the third floor, the porch was sagging. It had six long apartments, with two on each floor. Our apartment was on the top floor. This was our new home.

I do not know for sure how old this house was, but I'm guessing it was built before the Civil War. There was a secret, back stairway that my sisters and I later discovered. Taking it was like going on a scary adventure, perhaps like something in a Nancy Drew mystery. There was no heating system in this house and our new home was extremely cold. We had a coal stove in the kitchen and the heat from that stove was supposed to transfer to other rooms, but it did not. The steps leading to our apartment were steep and the ceilings were high.

My father rented the third floor apartment because the rent was the cheapest on this floor. Each apartment had six rooms that lined up from the front to the back of the house. The rooms were like a railroad car, one room led into the next. There were no doors on the rooms. You walked from one room to the next. Our house was two blocks from town. Our rent was only $15.00 a month. Perhaps my father would be able to pay this lower rent.

In 1941, my father decided things would be better if we moved from Monticello, NY to New York City. My mother and father took the 100-mile trip by bus to look things over. They rented an apartment at 108th and Central Park West for $50.00 per month. We moved to New York City during the fall of 1941. My father bought a small 1936 Ford Coupe for his transportation, but never took the rest of our family for a ride. He was accepted for employment in New York City working for Works Progress Administration (WPA).

My father loved President Franklin D. Roosevelt and his 'New Deal'. He said, "It was because of our President, I got this job." We were all very happy that our father was now working. To us, this was real success. He had a paying job doing construction work, by building some Army barracks at Fort Dix, New York.

We had a two-bedroom apartment on the third floor and had an elevator. The building had six floors, which was the tallest building we had ever seen. It was the first elevator my sisters and I had ever been on. It was slow, but extremely exciting.

This was the first time we ever had hot water and a warm house and it was wonderful to be able to take a hot bath. One of the bedrooms was for the girls. We had a double bed and three of us slept in that bed and another single bed where another sister slept. The entire room was filled with the two beds with only a very small space between them. I was fifteen at that time and attending high school.

On December 7, 1941, Pearl Harbor was

bombed. I remember that my father was smoking his cigar and listening to the news when the bombing was announced.

We now had all the conveniences. We had heat in every room, food to eat and life seemed to be going better. I took the subway to school. When I reached age 16, I was able to get working papers and a job. In my last two years of high school, I left my last class at 2:20pm, walked to my job and was sitting at my desk by 2:30pm doing clerical work for Longchamps Restaurants. I made 50 cents per hour and gave my mother most of the money until graduating from Straubenmueller Textile High School in 1946.

World War II was now over and so was my father's WPA job. My parents continued to live in New York for over twenty-five more years.

My mother went to work as a seamstress and sewed for the entire day. All the children in our family graduated from high school and moved away, just as I did in 1948. My oldest sister, Ruth moved to California a few years before I graduated. After graduation, I moved there, too.

In 1967, they moved to Oregon City, Oregon. They bought an old house near the railroad tracks. Both my father and mother were getting into their retirement years. My father never went to see a doctor for his entire life, because he did not believe in them.

In 1972, my mother called and told us the bad news. My father was not feeling well that day and his stomach seemed to be upset. She said he had been in the bathroom for a long time and decided to check on him to see if he was all right. She found him on the floor. He had fallen from the toilet stool. Apparently, he had a stroke and was dead at age seventy-four.

All of my brothers and sisters and I traveled to Oregon to be with our mother and help her with the funeral. My sisters and I looked through the important papers to see if we could find any insurance policies. There were none.

I called Uncle Harry, my father's rich brother in Los Angeles, to let him know that his brother died and that we were making funeral plans. He asked if there was any life insurance and I told him there was none. He said to let him know how much the funeral costs were and he would send my mother a check. We were overjoyed.

It was my job to make all the funeral arrangements, including picking out the coffin. The funeral director showed me the choices and I chose the one that was the lowest price. It was built of wood and painted an ugly dark green and inside was some inexpensive padded white material. The cost of the casket was $300. My father needed a new shirt and tie to be buried in. His suit coat seemed to be okay. The entire funeral cost was $800 and Uncle Harry sent mother the check and we were extremely thankful. Many people were at the funeral because my father belonged to the Odd Fellows Lodge and the members attended.

Many years in my life went by as I remembered being young, but never having a hug or a kiss from my father and I had no memories of hearing any loving words. I always resented the fact he never bought us anything new, not even a pair of shoes, and never having a doll when I was a little girl. I know now that it was not my father's fault we were poor children living during The Great Depression of the 1930's. It took me a long time to forgive my father for the things we did not have when we were growing up.

Whenever I smell the fragrance of a cigar or see paper sign painted with red and black letters, I remember him as an honest, non-drinking man that was always listening to the radio and maintaining his position as the boss of his family. That is my memory of my father.

The following was added to my paper. It is important because Monticello, NY, is in Sullivan County, where I was born. It is from a story from The New York Times, called "No One Has Starved." This sentence was not infrequently heard among people who were more financially comfortable, despite newspaper stories, such as this one: published on Christmas Eve., 1931. I came across it in the book <u>The Great Depression</u>, edited by David A. Shannon, Associate Professor of History, University of Wisconsin, A Spectrum Book, Prentice-Hall, Inc. Page 36 in the chapter America's Shame: The crisis of Relief.

"No One Has Starved."
Middletown, N.Y., Dec. 24, 1931

Attracted by smoke from the chimney of a supposedly empty summer cottage near Anwana Lake, in <u>Sullivan County</u>, Constable Simon Glasser found a young couple starving. Three days without food, the wife, who is 23 years old, was hardly able to walk. The couple, Mr. & Mrs. Wilfred Wild of New York, had been unemployed since their formerly wealthy employer lost his money, and several days ago they invested all they had, except 25 cents for food and bus fare to this region in search of work. Finding none, they went into this cottage, preferring to starve rather than beg. They said they had resigned themselves to dying together."

Another interesting item that was included in my term paper was a picture of President

Roosevelt returning with Mrs. Roosevelt from his Second Inauguration and under this picture was this article.

<u>A letter written to Mrs. Roosevelt from a six-teen-year old Michigan girl:</u>

"I am a high school girl and I must quit school because I am not dressed as other girls are. My clothes are all shabby from my dress to my shoes. Mrs. Roosevelt, would you kindly look among your things and see if there isn't something you can send me. Please don't let my parents find out that I wrote you asking you for help. I am decent and respectable and you know how some people are. They would laugh at me if they knew I wrote and asked you for old dresses." P 100, "<u>Growing Up in the Great Depression" by Richard Wormser</u>.

Stories Told To Me About The Great Depression

'Jake Edminster', who was age twenty at the time, was living at a logging camp in Itasca County, MN during the years of 1938 and 1939. He was working for $1.00 per day plus his room and board and worked six days a week. In the spring of 1939, the roads were bad because of the winter thaw and logs could not be moved.

Jake was without a job and returned home to live with his parents and four sisters and one brother. His mother was nearly blind and worked as a telephone operator. His father only milked six cows. They had no electricity, but did have a radio. Their farm was just 40 acres and located in Itasca City.

Sometimes they shot a deer out of season, skinned and butchered it and buried the hide and all the remains, so they would not get caught. But they would have meat for their family.

'Mel Brekkestran' lived on a farm in Gatzke, Marshall County, MN with thirteen kids in the family, seven sisters and six brothers. They had 40 acres. His dad worked for the city as a snowplow operator.

Mel told me his little brother, a first grader, and how they walked to school two miles each way. It was so cold during the winter and especially when the wind was blowing. Sometimes, his little brother would get tired and did not want to walk. He would lay down in the snow and cry. Mel had to carry him part way to school and he was a little boy too.

He said, "We had enough food to eat because we raised most of our food. The kid that lived near them came over our house often because he was

hungry and my mother always gave him something to eat."

When Mel was 11 years old, he learned to drive.
They had a new Ford, Model-T that cost them
$800.

'LeAna Jallo' was born in Minneapolis in 1917.
The family lived in northeast Minneapolis and she
had a younger brother. Her mother and father
built a new house before they were married. But
the house did not have a bathroom, no indoor
plumbing, no telephone and no electricity. They
heated their home with wood that was delivered
to them.

Her father first worked as a janitor for the
University of Minnesota. After that job, he worked
at the mill and took a streetcar to work. It was so
hot in the factory that the men worked in their
long underwear.

Jallo went to Silver Lake School where she often
played 'Jax'. They did not have a radio or a car. At
home, they too, ate oatmeal and a lot of potatoes.
Eggs sold for five cents per dozen, bread, five
cents a loaf. Horses pulled fire trucks as well as
delivering ice by horse and wagon. There were no
sidewalks.

'Mattie Moore' was born in Mississippi on
February 9, 1916. She had six sisters and was the
next to the oldest, in charge of milking seven

cows and feeding them. She chopped cotton when she was not milking. Her older sister was in charge of the cooking, the garden, the chickens and gathering eggs. Moore helped put up hay, cut soybeans and used a combine. She was from a family of sharecroppers. Their house was part of the payment for sharecropping.

'Shirley Goldberg', who was age eighty-six at the time of my interview with her, graduated from North High in 1929. The family lived on 8th Avenue, in north Minneapolis. She had three brothers and a sister. Her dad was a Hebrew teacher and was paid very little for this work. Shirley Goldberg was the next to the oldest sibling. She went to work as a bookkeeper for Brown's Plumbing Company earning $12.00 per week. She walked six blocks to work and always wore dresses. "I gave all $12 to my mother. The rest of the family worked and gave their pay to my mother, too. That was the only way we could pay our bills and have enough food to eat. If we did not have the money to pay the rent when it was due, the landlord waited for us to pay them when we could." She further said, "I used to wear hand-me-downs from my older sister." They heated their house with two stoves in different rooms and used coal and wood for heating.

Note: Jallo, Moore and Goldberg were residents at Lyndale Assisted Living, in Minneapolis, where I was doing a college Internship as a Program Manager.

In conclusion to my research project <u>"The People Tell Their Stories,"</u> I wrote the following:

The Great Depression of the 1930's was filled with years of endured hardships. The people of those times had many stories and the hardships they endured depended on what part of the country they lived in at that time, whether it was a town, city or farm. I spent hours at my computer and the library doing research and interviewed many people.

My instructor wrote the following note, making me extremely pleased. "Outstanding Paper! Your personal recollection and those of your sources point to the profound impact of this period of American History on your generation. This paper is also well-written and supported with ample information. Great job." (Course grade = A) /s/ Eric, Instructor.

Spider-Man
(The story as I remember it)

Several years ago, I was driving back from the shopping mall where I now work, and was listening to Public Radio. Diana Rheem was interviewing the creator of the comic book legend 'Spider-Man'. While initially, I was not all that interested in his story, I kept listening and the longer I listened, the more interested I became. The man sounded quite elderly and he was telling her about the times, when he was a little boy growing up in New York City, during the Great Depression.

He told her of his father, who became an unemployed He had been a ladies garment cutter but because of the depression, he was now without a job. He said that his father was extremely depressed and felt inadequate, because he could not support his family and they were often hungry. He told Diana Rheem that he did not have any toys to play with when he was a young boy and he created things to occupy his mind. He often played with insects and imagined that if one of these insects was big enough to become a kind of 'insect man', this creature could then save everyone from bad times and everything would be made good again.

However "Insect-Man" did not sound quite the way he thought it should for his hero. After a lot of insect and bug names, all of a sudden, he came up with "Spider-Man," and that had the right ring to it.

That was the way "Spider-Man" was first created. I was amazed with this story and I told myself this is almost the same story I could tell of growing up in the same state with an unemployed father and not enough to eat and no toys to play with. The young boy eventually became very successful and rich, because he turned his life into a creation that became a legend in comic books, collectable cards and in our time, an extremely successful movie.

This powerful story had me wish I were his friend when we were small children playing with insects and spiders and wishing for good things to happen and then I would be rich today, too.

On November 19th, 1995, I wrote an 'extra credit' eight-page report for my World War II History class, because I was failing this class and needed to do extra work to pass it. Even so, I liked history and the reason I enrolled in this class was because I never had the opportunity to learn about this war, when Japan bombed Pearl Harbor on December 7, 1941, I was a fourteen year-old student starting high school at that time and this current history was not in our textbooks. Taking this class helped me realize it was a terrible war.

Excerpts from My WWII Paper

[Editor's Note: The following story appears in its original unedited form.]

Franklin D. Roosevelt was our president when we entered WWII. Many countries were involved. Each country tried to out power another and Adolph Hitler was the dictator of Germany.

Hitler was attempting to conquer many countries as well as killing all the Jews. They did not fit into his plans of developing his Aryan, pure race. Some of the lucky Jews escaped and fled to other countries, including to the United States. Many were not and they were gassed to death in the 1940's.

According to information from World Book Encyclopedia, ["Hitler spread death as no person has done in modern history. "Have no pity! Act brutally!" he told his soldiers. He ordered tens of thousands of those who opposed him to be executed, and hundreds of thousands to be thrown into prison. Hitler particularly persecuted Jews. He ordered them removed and killed in countries he controlled. He set up concentration camps where about six million Jews were murdered. His emotional speeches made crowds cheer "Hiel, Hitler! "Holocaust was the systematic, state-sponsored murder of Jews and others by the Nazis during World War II (1939-1945). The Nazi dictator Adolf Hitler wanted to eliminate all Jews as part of his aim to conquer the world. The Nazis had killed about six million Jewish men, women, and children - more than two-thirds of the Jews in Europe."]

This history class required students to learn all the different generals names of numerous countries and the names of weapons, including guns, ships, tanks and airplanes. There was too much for me to learn and I became overwhelmed. I could never remember all the material the instructor required and was not passing his tests. He loved teaching World War II history and had been doing so for years. I asked him if I could interview some World War II veterans for extra credit and he said that I could.

I interviewed four veterans and Ralph Nieland's story was the most interesting one to me. Here is his story:

Ralph Nieland's Story

Ralph Nieland, age nineteen, was drafted into the Army Corps in 1942. He was tested at Fort Snelling, Minnesota to determine in what capacity he would be of most use, and his aptitude was toward mechanics and engineering. His basic training was held at Engineering School in Amarillo, and then he was off to Loredo, TX for Gunnery School. After six weeks, he was transferred to Salt Lake City, Utah to be assigned to the 453rd Bomb Group. After this required training, he was sent overseas to Attlebourgh, England at our U.S.A. bomber base. While there, Nieland was promoted to full-fledged engineer, T/Sgt. He was paid $96.00 per month and was placed as the team engineer with a crew of ten men.

At that time, the B-24 bomber Nieland's crew operated did not even have seat belts. He said, "We bombed Germany many times at Brunswick and Berlin, besides other places. On one mission, our plane was shot up so badly, the pilot was going to order the crew to bail out. Being the engineer, I was the one to over-ride him. As long as this plane will fly, we will keep flying it."

The plane was able to land back at its base and although it was shot up badly, no one was killed. He went on to say, "I was too chicken to bail out, I decided to keep our plane in the air. We tossed all our equipment out and managed to land. After that, our plane was taken to the graveyard for parts."

Nieland received the distinguished 'Flying Cross' for his over-all service in Germany. He was stationed in Germany and France for the better part of the year in 1944. He and his crew flew across the North Sea from Vincy, France to Germany and participated in thirty bombing missions. One of their planes was named 'Marshall Payment' to pay back Hitler for his misdeeds.

He went on to tell me what he called "The Horse Story." Their base was neighboring an English farmer's property and the people at the U.S. base were friends with the neighboring farmers. An English farmer's horse died and he was trying to decide what to do with his dead horse. The U.S. Air Corps wanted to be of assistance so they loaded up the dead horse in their airplane for the next mission to bomb Germany. They flew the 1,000-pound dead horse over Germany and dropped their bombs including the special gift of the dead horse.

Nieland had many stories to tell, but after four interviews and sixteen pages of notes, I had to conclude his story. He was medically discharged at age twenty-one with a severe case of ulcers In January of 1945.

I felt honored to have this opportunity to write about World War II. Hearing the Veterans stories first-hand, from the men that fought in this war and were still alive to tell their stories, made me proud to be a member of the VFW Post 494 in Crystal, MN. I did pass World War II history.

I worked at JCPenney Co. for ten years as a Sales Associate and one of my friends was Carmen Berlinerblau from Anoka, MN. We were both in the Shoe Department at this time and her daughter, Diana, age twelve, had to do a school project interviewing older persons about the 'old days' and I offered assistance by writing this:

I REMEMBER

[Editor's Note: The following story appears in its original unedited form.]

I remember being a little girl about your age, and then I grew up.

I remember weighing forty-eight pounds. I was skinny.

I remember eating oatmeal every day. I never eat oatmeal anymore.

I remember never having a doll and later in life, I became a doll collector.

I remember when a penny was a great deal. Anyone could buy a large lollipop for a penny.

I remember a dress I had with elastic in the middle. It was kind of ugly and was a 'hand-me-down' from someone. My parents could never afford to buy us new clothes. I was brought up during the depression years of the 1930's.

Many people were poor and unemployed. We were poor. That was a number of years after World

War I, and all the countries of the world were going through hard-times. All the years I was growing up, my family was going through hard-times.

I remember sleeping in a full-size bed with two of my sisters, and another sister slept in the other single bed. We had four kids in one bedroom.

I remember my first baby-sitting job during the summer. I was twelve and walked three miles each way to the summer resort where I took care of twins, and washed and ironed their clothes for $3.00 a week and worked six days each week. I gave my mother $2.50 and kept 50 cents for myself so I could buy things. The next summer, I took care of the same twins and got a raise to $5.00 per week; giving my mother $4.00 keeping $1.00 for myself.

I remember having a United States stamp collection. We had a fire in that room and my stamp collection burned with other things. Later in life, I became a stamp collector and continued collecting stamps for thirty-two years. I had a very large U. S. Mint collection, and loved my stamp-collecting hobby.

I remember my father having a small car. It could have been a 1936 model, but we never rode in the car while I was growing up. It was not until 1949 when I was married and learned to drive in a 1946 Nash Ambassador. I have been driving over forty-seven years.

I remember when I became a student-pilot in 1960. My youngest son, Greg, was age three, and mama was flying. I flew a small old 1946 Aeronca-Champ. I flew for twenty-two hours and did not get as far as I should for becoming a pilot. My son, Greg is a pilot for United Airlines, and has now become a Captain and flies the Airbus.

I remember World War II, and Pearl Harbor being bombed, but that was far away. I felt it was a bad thing, however, I really did not know much about that war.

I was a student in school, and remember when the war was over. I thought that was great. "The war was over." That's all I knew about this war. Now I'm in college and finished taking a history class on World War II, and that is when I learned how bad that war was.

I remember when President Kennedy was shot and how awful that was. Everyone was constantly listening to the news for a long time regarding the assassination of our President.

I remember Jackie Kennedy. She was the prettiest and youngest and thinnest President's wife we ever had. All the women were paying close attention to the new fashions Jackie Kennedy started. The ladies all wanted Jackie Kennedy 'hair-dos' and her style of clothing became the very fashionable kind of clothes to wear. I liked Jackie Kennedy.

Times have changed so much. Today, I am very conservative about many things in my life, and appreciate things that others do not. Thank you, Diana, for letting me remember some 'old times' and writing this paper for you.

Part III
Stories From
My Married Years

The following was written on 1/27/98 for a
memoir writing class.

*[Editor's Note: The following story appears in its original unedited
form.]*

The Wedding

The white-lace ankle-length dress, wide rimmed hat, the 3 inch platform heels, and the corsage of red roses was what the long dark-haired, short, nervous bride-to be, was wearing. The 5'6" light complexioned red-haired young man dressed in his two-piece official Navy white uniform was the groom.

It was Friday the 10th

day of June 1949 in the Chapel of the U. S. Naval Air Station of Whiting Field, Florida, 4:00p.m and this very important day was about to happen. It was "The Wedding."

Petty Officer, Third Class, Cliff Chandler had to put in for 'special liberty' that weekend because he had 'the duty'. On the form, it requested reason for 'special liberty' and he put down, "Getting married." It was a usual hot June day in the Chapel. The small group gathered including the Chaplain, the Best Man, Cliff's best friend, Petty Officer First Class, James P. Dugas, Mary Cowden, Matron of Honor, worked with Cliff in the office and was a civil service employee. A Chief gave me away. We were both extremely nervous.

Our parents could not be with us. It was too far for them to travel and they could not afford the trip. Cliff's family was from Minnesota and my family was from New York.

Before the wedding, Cliff and I rented a small apartment in the Town of Milton, Florida. It was located seven miles from the base. Our entrance to our small one bedroom apartment was in the rear of the house where our friends, Joe and Louise English lived. Our first home is where we were going to spend the beginning of our marriage. Cliff did not have any military leave to go on a honeymoon.

And the wedding ceremony began and soon ended. "Will you love, honor and obey" were some of the words I seem to remember. I was crying and could hardly talk. When the Chaplain said, "I pronounce you husband and wife," I felt better. It was over. I was okay.

"You may kiss the bride now." Yes, we were married and I was the bride. We planned and took our wedding party to Fort Walton, FL, which is on the north west coast of Florida. The sand on the beach was white and beautiful. We had a delicious dinner served with champagne and great music. The words to the song the band played were, "Oh how we danced on the night we were wed" and Cliff and I danced.

After a few hours, we all drove approximately 50 miles back to Milton, FL. We were now husband and wife and we were going home to our new apartment.

My rose corsage soon died and I put it in a book to press it forever.

My oldest sister, Ruth, was an artist and she painted a portrait of me in my white-lace wedding dress in oil on canvas. She did this portrait from a photo I sent her. I received this rolled painted canvas a number of years after Cliff and I was married. I never had this portrait framed.

Approximately six months after our marriage, Cliff and I did go on a honeymoon. We drove to Cliff's family home in MN so I could meet everyone and they could meet me. I was nervous again. We drove our 1946 pea-green Nash Ambassador from Milton, FL to Cushing. They lived on this large spacious area with old buildings, a little log cabin type old house and it was a farm.

All his relatives were farmers and always in the barn. I was never on a farm before and was the only person that was ever seen holding their nose when entering a barn.

Joe & Florence Chandler

Later, Cliff told me no one ever holds his or her nose when going into a barn. That is good farm air fragrance coming from those cows.

Many times Cliff would introduce me to his friends or relatives as, "This is the bride." I liked that especially after we were married for a number of years.

Cliff and I became the parents of three sons and grandparents of five. He retired from the Navy after 20 years of military service. We had lived in the States of FL, VA, RI, ND, CA, and MN. When Cliff retired from the U. S. Navy as a Chief Yeoman, we made our home in Minnesota.

We did many things together including traveling to Germany, Spain, France, Hawaii, Jamaica, Mexico and Canada. We flew our own small planes from the airstrip on our farm to many places in the states. We went boating, fishing, dancing, and traveled in our motor home all over the country, and kept working.

During a period of 20 years, we had small family-owned businesses including a sales lot for manufactured housing, an insurance agency, a satellite and video store, two small mobile home parks, a small motel, and lived on a 100- acre farm. We raised 40 head of Beefalo, and had one very ugly buffalo on the farm for a period of four years. We never stopped working.

James P. Dugas, - Best Man

The Best Man at our wedding on June 10, 1949 was James P. Dugas. James has now retired from the U. S. Navy as a Chief Warrant Officer, after thirty years of service. Jim Dugas had loved the Navy.

Our friendship with him has continued over the years. We named our first son, James after James Dugas.

Many years after Cliff was retired from the Navy in 1965, we started to visit Jim Dugas at his home in Florida. At that time, he lived on his ranch with another retired Navy Man, his friend, Jerry Spicer. They each resided in their respective mobile homes. Jerry Spicer lived with his wife, Ruth and her four children. Jim and Jerry shared a garage that they had built together, which included a workshop and a washer and dryer. Jim loved to tinker around in the garage for many hours each day. He had a radio, where he spent many hours listening to classical music, a fan and whatever else he needed to make working in his garage a happy experience.

On a number of occasions, we drove our motor home to his Florida ranch for our winter vacations. We would park our motor home, hook it up to Jim's water and sewage system and stay as long as three weeks at a stretch. I did the cooking in the motor home and Jim ate with us each day we were there. He cooked a meal for us in his own kitchen every few days and brought it with him to our motor home for our communal meals. Jim liked to call me 'Sis'.

I observed that Jim had a consistent daily routine. He did all his house and yard work in the morning, then changed into good, squeaky-clean casual clothes and joined his VFW buddies at the VFW Hall for an afternoon beer and discussion. He said that he did that routine most every day. His military family expected him to show up. They were a major part of Jim's life.

Jim had married a Japanese gal while stationed

in Japan. They had twin daughters. He had been divorced for some time and we never met his girls, but he loved them dearly.

On September 14, 2000 at 12:05 a.m., Jim died of terminal cancer of the brain. Here are parts of what his niece, Barbara Callaghan, emailed to her friends and relatives. Cliff received this email and sent me a copy. Listed below is a portion of this email:

"He was doing fine and was being a 'perfect gentleman patient'. He took a severe turn on Wednesday morning, which required us to call for the Hospice nurse. When Jim passed away he was surrounded with family and lots of love. We had his favorite Brahms classical music playing and he was being cuddled and hugged the entire time. He was in no pain and went gently."

"Our friends adopted him and they all called him "Uncle Jim." His daughters, Mary and Margie, came for a wonderful visit. We had all been out of touch with each other for over 30 years. It was a warm but sad reunion. Jim was very excited to see the girls and they smothered him with love and attention the entire time."

"When Jim had company, a lot of Pat's police friends, he would talk a lot about his friend's back home and his service years. He loved everyone at the "V" (VFW) and said his friends there were so kind to him and he missed them all. In closing, we are having a send off for Jim tonight at dusk at the VA Cemetery in Danville, IL."

"We are going to the Navy monument and the minister will be there to attend. We will say our prayers, release a white balloon and then we are going to 'pop' a Miller Lite™ in his honor while playing 'Anchors Away."

I hope you all join us in prayer at 5:30 p.m., Illinois time to give him a glorious send off. Jim was a special person and will be missed by many for a long time.

Sincerely,

Patrick and Barbara Callighan

Clifford and our son, Gregory went to the Bloomington, IL hospital to visit with Jim Dugas before he died. I too, will always remember Jim Dugas, and he will always be our 'Best Man'.

This was originally written for a Memoir Writing Class on January 13, 1998

Wanting To Solo As A Student Pilot

It all began on February 21, 1960. At the time, I was the wife of a U. S. Navy career man and a private pilot. It was at Montgomery Air-Field, San Diego, CA, where I became a student pilot. My youngest son, Greg, was three at that time. Today, Greg is a Captain with United Airlines.

On that first day of flight training, I flew with my instructor in 1946 Aerona Champ. It was a two-place private plane, known as a tail-dragger, because it had two wheels in front and one in the back. A Navy flying club, called the 'Flying Swabbies' owned this airplane. I was the only female student pilot in their club, becoming eligible for membership because my husband, Clifford was a member. My first lesson lasted 45 minutes and as it says in my logbook, I was flying straight and level.

During the month of October 1960, I flew more hours than any other member of the club and was getting anxious to solo, which means that I would fly the airplane by myself, with the instructor safe and sound on the ground. My instructor said, "When I think you are ready, I will let you know."

I had a few problems. The Aeronca Champ was not built for short women. I had trouble reaching the rudders and needed cushions under and behind me to reach them. It was almost a problem to fasten the seat belt. I liked flying 'the left-hand pattern' and using a certain runway. One day, the wind was coming from a different direction and everyone had to take off and land on a different runway, using a right-hand pattern. That disturbed me very much. I did not fly well for that lesson. A good pilot could fly out of any runway and in any pattern.

Today, they were using my runway and I decided it was a good day to solo. I called the instructor to ask him if I could. He said that he would come to the airport to give me another flight lesson and he would be the one to make the decision of whether or not I would solo.

We took off - my take-off was great and the flight around the airport was okay with one exception, three planes were in the pattern. I had to stay in position, taking my turn to land. I was quite far from the landing strip and also quite low. The other planes landed and now it was my turn. I was very close to the field and 'lined up' right where I was supposed to be. However, I seem to have pulled the nose up, causing the aircraft to stall drop prematurely. We barely made it onto the airstrip. This caused this the airplane to bounce a few times. The instructor had to take the controls to get the plane on the ground. He then said, "Let's go around the pattern again."

I took off again and it went better. Up into the

sky we flew and then I leveled off at the proper time. I was going around the pattern and a strong, crosswind started. A good pilot knows to fly into the wind to correct for any crosswind. I knew that and did it correctly. I was coming in for my landing lined up right in the middle of the runway where I was supposed to be. Only one thing went wrong. The aircraft did not stay on the ground and we bounced again and again, totaling three times. My instructor had to assist me with my landing, and said, "Let me take you around the pattern."

I was crying. I said, "Maybe, anyone like me, that can not fly a plane any better than I did, should not fly." After twenty-two hours logged in my flight logbook, I never flew again as a student pilot.

By 1974, my youngest son, Greg, was a pilot. He had his Private Pilot license and Instructor's License. Greg and I flew in our two-seat, tail dragger, 'Luscombe.' We took off from our private airstrip, which Clifford and his father hit built years ago on our farm property. We were heading for Purdue University where Greg was going to begin college, majoring in 'Pilot Air Technology' to become a commercial pilot and hopefully fly for a major airline company.

I flew with Greg for many hours as we crossed Minnesota, Wisconsin and Illinois. Since Greg had his Instructor's License, I was hoping he could fill in my own pilot's logbook, thus resuming my status as a student pilot. The only problem was that I had lost my logbook years ago. I am glad that I finally found it to prompt my memory for this story.

I now only have joyous memories of my student pilot experiences and no regrets for the experience I gained. For many years when my children were younger, our family flew everywhere with Cliff as the pilot and me as the co-pilot and it was my job to keep the airplane straight and level.

The following segment was written on Valentine's Day on February 14, 1998 for a memoir writing class although on February 14, 2003, I added a little more content.

As Time Goes By

[Editor's Note: The following story appears in its original unedited form.]

On June 10, 1949 these two 21 year olds, the young man being the oldest by one day, their astrology sign being Virgo, were married.

A few years later on May 25, 1952 at the United States Naval Hospital in Portsmouth, VA, another important event took place. A 6 lb, 14 oz. baby boy arrived in the world. He was named James Donald

Chandler. I was happy, scared, and extremely tired, and new at this mother-thing. The new daddy was happy and pleased to have our son.

Cliff was stationed on a small Navy ship called a 'Destroyer.' His ship was docked in Newport News, VA. Every other week, Cliff would come home on liberty. We lived in a small mobile home in Portsmouth, VA.

On May 4, 1954, it was time for me to return to the Portsmouth Naval Hospital to have Richard Joseph, a little guy, weighing in at 7 lbs., 4 oz. When Richard was very young, I returned to work as a clerk-typist for Civil Service at the St. Julien's Creek Ammunition Depot. My job was to accurately type ammunition reports. Cliff continued to have 'Sea Duty' aboard the Destroyer.

In 1956 and we were residents of Fargo, ND. Cliff was on recruiting duty. On September 19, 1956, Gregory Allen, our 7 lb., 11 oz. son was welcomed on board the Chandler family. Our family unit was complete.

We not only had a new baby in Fargo, but also purchased our first home equipped with a piano. No one in our family played the piano, but unless we bought the piano, the owner would not sell us her house. Now we had our first home and the piano.

This house was the one we could afford on our Navy budget. This great old piano sat in our living room taking up space, but we grew to appreciate it until I decided to take piano lessons. We also purchased our first new furniture, a White-Ash, bedroom set. Now we had our first home, an old piano and rocker she wanted to sell for $50.00. I was working full-time for Penn Mutual Life Insurance Company, and trying to be a mother too with limited time. Life was good.

I took a number of piano lessons, but practicing was a problem due to the lack of time. The lesson I was to learn was 'Three Blind Mice', which sounded awful and soon Daddy and our little boys ganged up on me, deciding their mommy should quit learning to become a piano player and that was the end of my lessons, but the piano remained.

Some time in 1956, there was a terrible tornado heading towards Fargo, which touched down approximately one street away. I was at the grocery store doing the weekly shopping and it looked like a bad storm was coming our way. Cliff was home with our four-month baby Greg. Everyone in the store seemed to be clearing out, but I still had my groceries to pay for and then I was heading home.

Young Chandler Family

59

When arriving home, it was quiet and could not find Cliff and the baby and did not know why. I finally heard Cliff calling me to come down to the basement and was overwhelmed with the fact that Cliff had our baby in the basement. Never being involved with a tornado, I did not know that was where we were supposed to be. A few minutes after, we heard this gigantic loud noise like freight trains coming right over our house and we were nearly hit.

This tornado wiped out an entire section of Fargo called West Fargo that took years to rebuild. I learned from that day, tornadoes are extremely dangerous and storm warnings valuable. Now I have the greatest respect for all storms and am extremely afraid of tornadoes and other types of severe weather. My home I now live in has a basement and that gives me some peace.

When working for Penn Mutual Life Insurance Company doing clerical work, I had some desire to become an Insurance Representative. My boss said, "No, women did not sell insurance. They did the office work and only men sold insurance." Our lives seemed very busy. Our sons were growing, I was working and Cliff was on recruiting duty.

In 1956, we were transferred to San Diego. Cliff was again, on 'Sea Duty'. Our first brand new three-bedroom home with two baths was purchased. I worked at Juvenile Hall as an Admissions' Clerk for the next four years and always had good baby sitters so could continue working. Navy pay was not great, so two incomes helped us buy things we could not otherwise afford. In 1961, Cliff received his orders for recruiting duty to Minneapolis. Our three sons and all our stuff we bought since being married seemed to be making these moves more difficult. Cliff loved this move because he was being transferred home to MN.

We bought a home in Crystal, and again, I went to work this time for a general contractor, Mark Z. Jones II, and later became office manager. While Cliff was still in the Navy, we both became Security and Life Insurance Licensed to sell mutual funds and life insurance. Cliff was recruiting during the day and doing some sales work in the evenings.

Some evenings I had appointments to show mutual funds and life insurance plans to prospects and often would come home with a sale and a great feeling of accomplishment. I loved to sell the idea of these plans and never sold anything that would make a person rich. The theory used was based on "Do you think you will be better off with this plan because you put some money away for twenty years from now?" My love for selling the idea of systematic savings made me one of the top sales representatives of a mostly male sales force.

Our Hamiliton Manager, Ralph Zabel wanted me to quit working for Mark Z. Jones because the opportunity was greater working full time as a sales representative selling financial services. The decision to quit working there had been made. While trying to tell Mark Jones my wishes to resign because the future was better in financial sales, the state of being terribly upset brought me to near tears. Mark Jones went on to tell me he would raise my salary from $400.00 to $500.00 per month because of becoming a valuable team player. Still not able to talk because I was going to cry, no answer. When not answering, he then said, "Okay, I'll give you $600.00 per month and work you like hell." That was the time I got a big raise to staying. That night Ralph and Fran Zabel invited Cliff and I for dinner to celebrate my leaving Mark Z. Jones II to become a full time securities representative. That did not happen and I had to tell them, I would not be leaving Mark Z. Jones because I got a big raise from $400.00 to $600.00 per month was a big deal at that time for someone without college.

Another time, Cliff and I were attending a dinner being held by a Professional Sales School. It was a class Cliff had taken and it was an important event with mostly male persons participating. An Insurance Instructor across the table from us was with one of his students. I decided to tell them I sold life insurance and had made three sales that week. He asked me, "What insurance company do you work for?" Our Securities company just switched insurance companies and could not think of the name of the new company. I hedged a little and then said to Cliff, "What insurance company do we work for?" Cliff was a little embarrassed and told them.

This story got back to our manager and at the monthly meeting, and after turning in my business written, our manager said, "Some people here do not know who the hell they work for but they still turn in business."

Cliff retired from the Navy at age 37 in 1965 and the family was invited to attend. We were all proud to be present at this official Navy Ceremony. Chief Petty Officer, Clifford J. Chandler was being 'Piped out of the Navy'.

Cliff wanted me to continue to work for Mark Z. Jones because we needed the money. After retiring Cliff took several new jobs of selling insurance, airplanes and radio systems and decided he wanted to have his own business up north.

In 1968, Cliff decided to go into business for himself, moving up north to Little Falls, MN started C & M Homes, Inc., which was sales and service of manufactured housing. Every weekend, I would drive north with our sons to join Cliff and help with his new business. After doing this for nearly one year, decided to leave my good job and move north.

In 1969, I did resign at the time I was earning $800.00 per month and was in the process of negotiating for $1,000.00 per month. However, I thought it was time for me, and our sons to join their Dad. It was a huge decision when I decided to resign from my job and move our family to Little Falls and be together and I could assist Cliff.

From a large house in Crystal, we were now living on our sales lot in a two-bedroom, 12' x 60' mobile home. This was not only Cliff's home, but also his office and was much too small for our family. We had to sacrifice many of our previous comforts to our new business life. Later we had a 24' x 52', three-bedroom doublewide, modular home set up on our sales lot for the next six years. Everyone knows the old saying, "Home is where the heart is." We should have adapted a new saying for the Chandlers and it would be "Home is where our sales lot is."

During the summer of 1975, we moved again on our 100-acre farm in Cushing, MN. We moved into our new three-bedroom, modular home. It was set up on a full basement and had a two-car attached garage. Our new home was very nice and had been professionally decorated. We were now living 18 miles away from our sales lot continuing C & M Homes for 13 years before selling it.

At one time, we raised 40 head of 'Beefalo' and one baby buffalo, which was given to him by one of his Masonic lodge brothers serving on the Board for the Little Falls Zoo. He thought Cliff should have that baby buffalo on our farm. Besides owning the baby buffalo, we also owned the Innsbrook Motel, the Randall Mobile Home Park, and the Pierz Mobile Estates in Pierz. We went into the Insurance Business, one office in Randall and the other in Rice. Our son, Richard, owned and operated the Rice agency. We later had a Satellite and Video Store. We also owned several small business buildings along with some contract for deeds and other rental property. We never stopped working.

Stamp Collecting
An Important Part of My Life

Chandler's presentation at the Randall

I started collecting stamps in 1959 and never stopped until 1991. It was important for me to buy what are known as 'U. S. Mint' stamps. I started with plate blocks, which were blocks of four stamps with the sheet number printed along the side of the block of four stamps. During this time, The United States Post Office [USPO] also started putting the Zip Symbol on each pane of stamps. I then added both, the plate blocks and the zip code blocks to my collection.

Each time a new stamp was introduced by the USPO, I was one of the first collectors at the Post Office, making sure to purchase the new plate blocks. One of the first things you learn when you are a U. S. stamp collector is that you get to know the local Postmaster. The Postmaster in Randall MN was Lyle Nelson and after he retired, Roxanne Judkins.

I then became interested in what are called 'First Day Covers'. A cover is an envelope with a picture on the upper left-hand corner, commemorating the stamp. The covers that were very colorful and more expensive and had beautiful pictures on them were called 'silk covers'. Those were the covers were the ones I bought.

Later, I became interested in collecting full panes of U. S. Stamps. Those were more costly. My obsession with stamps became one of the most important things in my life and bought entire collections from others if they were affordable.

In 1962, I started my two sons, Jim and Richard with collecting stamps. They did not share my enthusiasm for stamp collecting and when they told me they were going to sell their collections, I bought their collections for $20.00 each and still have both of their limited world stamp collections.

On the wall of my office, I have two large beautifully framed collections of Duck Stamps dating from 1935 through 1984. I drove several hundred miles to northern Minnesota for an auction to buy these framed Duck Stamps. Another person was bidding against me and I got them for $300.00 and was delighted.

The other framed display of stamps over my desk is the 'Charles A. Lindbergh 50th Anniversary' collection, designed by the <u>Minnesota Historical Society</u> and issued in a limited collection of just two hundred sets. It was made available for sale on May 21, 1977, the same day that the USPO released the Charles A. Lindbergh Stamp and their 'First Day Cover', which I purchased at the Little Falls MN Post Office. (Little Falls was the boyhood home of Charles Lindberg.)

A milk can outfitted with a vinyl seat, which I painted black is also part of the office collection. I 'mod-podged' 'cancelled' (already used postage) U.S. Commemorative Stamps all over the milk can. It is one of my proudest possessions along with the framed stamp collections.

When divorced in 1991, my stamp collection was extensive and valuable. I was afraid it could be lost from fire or theft in my apartment building. I decided the best thing I could do with my stamps was to sell them. I checked on the value of my collection with a large stamp auction dealer. After looking over my collection, it was decided that because I had an enormous collection of United States Mint, to break up these mint stamps into three different lots. He told me that if we spaced the sale of my mint collection a few weeks apart, the mint stamps would go for higher values. I had to do a lot of work and line them up into lots of approximately $100.00 of the actual mint value, so the auctioneer would know what he had to have for reasonable bids.

All stamp auctions are always advertised in advance to bring in the interested stamp collectors in what will be auctioned. I attended all of the auctions. At one of them, my Presidential-Collection was on the block. I decided I wanted it back. I had to bid against another bidder to get this collection back plus pay the auction fee besides. I have that collection today. After the three auctions, I came out with $10,000.00 for my stamp collection, which I immediately invested for retirement. I have never completely let go of my love for stamp collecting.

In May 1987, Mary Donnelly, the Editor of a small publication called the Advisor, wrote a story of my stamp collecting activities. I have included some of this article here:

"A lot of history can be learned from being a stamp collector and instead of buying candy, buy stamps. That way you won't get any cavities either," Chandler said. "I save stamps every single day," she told the children. The Benjamin Franklin Stamp Club was started as a public service of the postal department and former Postmaster Lyle Nelson started the club for the children in

Randall. Chandler encouraged the students to start young and continue collecting. Her collection became both a hobby as well as a retirement plan but keeps doing it because she is hooked.

Did Tiny Tim's Singing "Tip-Toe Through The Tulips" Cause Our Big Building To Fall?

On our mobile and modular home sales lot, we had a large pole building, which we used for storage. In the early 1970's, this building collapsed, during a late evening storm, while we were watching NBC's 'Tonight Show' with Johnny Carson. His guest for the evening was 'Tiny Tim'. The big news was that he was announcing his marriage to his fiancée, 'Miss Vicky.'

Tiny Tim was a tall man, with long straight black hair, hanging below his shoulders. He had a distinctive nose, and appeared to be in his 40's. Miss Vicky was short and quite young. I do not know if that match was made in heaven or not. Love is complicated.

I do remember a loud noise out on our sales lot during this bad storm, which sounded like something crashing while Tiny Tim was in the middle of singing his famous song, "Tip-Toe through the Tulips," while also playing his famous ukulele. The weather was too severe to go out on the lot that evening, so we decided to wait until morning.

On the next morning, it was not good news. Our building had indeed collapsed during the storm and the roof was completely caved in. The only thing I could think of doing was to write to Johnny Carson and tell him what had happened to our roof while Tiny Tim was singing his famous song, thinking it would be interesting information.

Finally, after quite a few weeks, I received a letter back from 'The Tonight Show'. It was a short, one sentence letter that for me was disappointing. No one had read my letter. I do not even think it was opened. I believe, a staff member just put all his fan mail in one pile, and the answer I received was this: "Thank you for your interest in the Johnny Carson Show." I never wrote Johnny Carson another letter.

Some offers were made to Cliff to buy our caved-in building for scrap metal, but he refused all offers. He said, "I'm going to put the building back up again." With a crew of a few workers and a lot of slow persistent work, Cliff did restore the building to a stronger state than previously and deserved significant credit for his determination to succeed with that enormous project.

Hubert H. Humphrey
A Few Days Before He Died

On January 3, 1978, I received a short personal letter from Hubert Humphrey. It was hand signed by him. One week later, he died.

I was extremely proud of this letter and have kept it for years. I had 'modge-podged' a picture of him and his wife, Muriel onto a small rock and sent it to them.

[Editor's note: What I personally find interesting about this story is that both my father and mother had always been a staunch Republicans. As a kid, I remember many instances of hearing her voice strong, negative opinions about Governor, Senator and finally Vice President Hubert Humphrey.

Mom had been doing a lot of 'modge-podging', which is where one took photos or pictures from magazines and pasted them onto other surfaces such as rocks, by using a thick, clear plastic-like material that is painted on.

Many Minnesotans were moved by Hubert Humphrey's fight with cancer and my mom was emotionally empathetic enough to go beyond her political opinions and reach out based on the human feelings we all have when facing grave terminal disease and death.]

United States Senate

WASHINGTON, D.C. 20510

January 3, 1978

Ms. Millie Chandler
Route 1
Cushing, Minnesota   56443

Dear Millie:

Just a brief note to thank you so much
for the paper weight which you made for
us for Christmas.

You were so kind to remember us, and we
are sincerely grateful to you.

Best wishes for a Happy New Year.

Sincerely,

Hubert H. Humphrey

Hubert H. Humphrey

United States Senate

WASHINGTON, D.C. 20510

OFFICIAL BUSINESS

Hubert H. Humphrey

U.S.S.

Ms. Millie Chandler
Route 1
Cushing, Minnesota   56443

This article came over the came over the Web:
www.rrstar.com
e-mail: rrscopydesk@smtp.registertartower.com
(The Associated Press)

73

In the Rockford Star Sunday paper during the month of July of 2002, this Associated Press article appeared.

Hubert H. Humprey's desk sold at garage sale

Orono, Minnesota. – From diehard Democrats to scavengers, hundreds of people snapped up a slice of Minnesota history Thursday at a garage sale held by Hubert H. Humphrey's youngest son.

Up for grabs were the former vice president and the U. S. senator's camouflage hunting vest, campaign memorabilia and a desk he used in the Senate. The desk was priced at $10,000

Some people waited more than an hour to get inside, but there were few complaints.

Humphrey was elected to the Senate in 1948 and served as vice president under Lyndon B. Johnson. He lost the 1968 presidential election to Richard Nixon and returned to the Senate in 1971.

His wife, Muriel, was appointed to serve out the rest of his term. She died in 1998.

The closet thing to a "museum-quality piece was the desk. Another son, Skip, lost the governor's race in 1998 to Jesse Ventura.

. . . .

Sometime in 2003, there was an antique show at Machesney Park Mall and I was lucky enough to find and purchase some great posters drawn by <u>Norman Rockwell</u> in 1968. One was of Presidents Reagan, Nixon, and Johnson and another was of Bobby Kennedy, Eugene McCarthy and "yes, one of Hubert Humphrey."They have all been mounted on my basement walls. I had purchased one more of Martin Luther King, Jr. photographed by 'Cal Bernstein', for <u>Look Magazine,</u> in the 1960's.

The Geof Steiner Story – Honoring Viet Nam War Soldiers

Sometime prior to 1987, Cliff and I knew Geof Steiner, because he was a friend of our retired Navy friends, Joe and Ruth Lussier. Geof was a veteran of the Viet Nam War and wanted to honor his fellow soldiers.

He decided to plant a tree for every US soldier who died in the war and a second group of trees for those US soldiers missing in action. The trees were to be planted on his land near Cushing, Minnesota. He went to several agencies in Morrison County Minnesota, looking for funds to purchase the trees. Soon this was soon making news with both local and later the national media.

Our Minnesota Senator of the time, Rudy Boschwitz, became involved and here is the rest of the story.

On November 30, 1987, the United States White House had written the following letter to Geof Steiner. You also see the picture of Steiner and his wife, taken with President Reagan and Senator Rudy Boschwitz, taken at The White House. He was proud of his visit with the President and gave me a copy of the letter and picture.

THE WHITE HOUSE
WASHINGTON

November 30, 1987

Dear Mr. Steiner:

It was a pleasure meeting you when you came to the White House with Senator Boschwitz -- and thank you very much for presenting me with the official flag of the Bicentennial of the United States Constitution. I particularly appreciate this special remembrance and the related items which you brought for me.

I am most grateful for your dedicated efforts to memorialize the Americans killed in action during the Vietnam war. Your selfless determination to plant a tree in honor of each of these brave Americans and those still missing in action is most commendable. You have my best wishes as you carry out this patriotic mission.

Sincerely,

Ronald Reagan

Mr. Geoffrey Steiner
The Living Memorial Trust Fund
Route 1, Box 398
Cushing, Minnesota 56443

'To Geof Steiner'
with best wishes, Ronald Reagan.

His mission of planting all those trees has been accomplished and the honored Vietnam soldiers have become part of the natural beauty of the woods in Cushing, Minnesota. I am pleased to have known Geof Steiner and am proud of how one person can make a difference, by honoring the lives and memories of our fallen and missing Vietnam War soldiers. For me, this was an important Vietnam War story and there is nothing as beautiful as a tree.

Uncle Ed Bates
An Important Person In My Life

Every person has fond memories of their family and Clifford's Uncle Ed and his wife Mildred were part of my life. When my sons were growing up, their great Uncle Ed and Aunt Mildred's farm was their favorite place to visit. She would have the most generous assortment of food on their dinner table, which was part of the joy of the visit. Mildred would play the piano or organ in the front room and while she played,

Uncle Ed told us about 'the old days'.

For their 50th Anniversary, I wrote a skit about Uncle Ed and Aunt Mildred's life, which was performed by the Bates' close friends and neighbors, Jim and Mary Skoog.

Cliff and I took Ed and Mildred on their first and only out of state trip to see their relatives and what a trip it was. We traveled in our motor-home and Ed recorded the events of trip on a cassette tape recorder each day. With his recording, he said that he was able to relive that trip many times. It was a great experience for us all.

Soon after their 50th Anniversary, Mildred developed Alzheimer's disease and spent the next few years in a nursing home. Uncle Ed visited her every single day, fed her, and watched her grow worse. She always seemed to know me when I visited her. I made a special pillow for her that she kept on her bed. Ed moved into her room to be with her. She died after a number of years and Ed remained in the Nursing Home and kept the pillow I made for Mildred on his bed.

The Morrison County Record published this story on July 5, 1998.

(Morrison County Record Editor's Note: The following article was written by Millie Chandler, formerly of Randall, as part of a journalism assignment, about

Millie, Mabel and her son Calvin with 100th birthday quilt

Mabel Sanders following her 100th birthday in 1997. Mabel Sanders recently passed away and the article is printed in her memory.)

Going To See Mabel Sanders

Mabel's quilt was sitting on a special rack and she proudly said, "That's my new quilt my granddaughter, Maureen, made for my hundreth birthday." It represented the life of her memories for this pleasant, white-haired lady, wearing a cotton print dress, with a blue cardigan sweater, as she sat in her rocker watching her "soaps." It did not seem to matter that her hearing was not good.

Mabel Sanders resides approximately 100 miles north of Minneapolis on the Camp Ripley road outside the village of Randall. In Little Falls, this summer, a nursing home resident, Ed Bates, said, "Mabel Sanders is one hundred years old. She is a tough old gal."

Sanders reside in the home that was originally built by her deceased husband, Paul, and her sons in 1947. Her husband died in 1950, leaving Mabel with her nine children to raise. Three of her children are now deceased. She took over the family business, Sanders Trucking, and ran it for fifty years doing the bookwork and answering the phones. They hauled cattle to St. Paul Stock Yards, two or three times a week.

Her oldest son is now seventy-five and her youngest daughter, sixty-nine, has twenty-four grandchildren and did not remember if she has six or seven great grandchildren. When Sanders was asked when she was born, she said, "I was born but do not remember when." She laughed and everyone joined in laughter with her. Calvin proudly said, "My mother was born on May 2, 1897, and is now one hundred years plus five months."

Sanders still enjoys playing bingo two or three times each week. She plays two cards for each game and sometimes she wins. She said, "Just the other night, I won $30." She enjoys eating out. She said, "One of my favorite places to eat is Ed's Place in Motley because they give senior discounts." She reads the paper daily. She does not take any vitamins and enjoys eating whatever she desires, walks with a cane and goes to bed when tired. A Nurses' aide from Little Falls comes to her home about twice a week to do some cleaning and assists her with bathing.

She said, "Everything is so different than it was." The memories kept alive by the treasured quilt showed photos reproduced on material. The photos included Mabel's life as a young bride and many important family pictures. This treasured quilt will probably be passed on to other family members as time goes by. Just a quilt and memories is what 100 years of living may be all about.

Cruising Down the River with 'The Lida Rose'

For some years, Cliff took many trips with our twenty-three foot Fiberform brand boat, his first larger fishing boat, to one of the best for salmon fishing destinations, just out of Two Harbors, Wisconsin. He went on a number of fishing outings with his buddies. Cliff was very good at salmon fishing and was always bringing home a good catch. The salmon were great eating.

The Lida Rose was the name of our beautiful boat that Cliff decided to buy, once he read the ad. It was twenty-three foot long and the bow of the boat had enclosed living quarters. It had a large bed inside the hull of the boat, dining seating, a stove, refrigerator, counter space, windows and a toilet. In the stern or back of the boat, there was a smaller area that could accommodate sleeping for up to two more people. In the upper portion of the boats center, there was the cockpit, where the steering was located. Yes, we had needed to upgrade our boat.

It was a seasoned, much traveled watercraft with a previous history. There had been a published story featuring this boat and the previous owners' journeys in an outdoor sporting magazine.

This boat was great and I know Cliff loved it. He dreamed of taking this boat on a long Mississippi River journey from Minnesota to the Gulf of Mexico. He frequently talked about the two of us "going down the Mississippi River."

There was only one thing wrong with his dream. I was extremely fearful of water and stormy turbulent weather and told Cliff I would not go on that trip with him unless added to the boat training he already had by attending a certified watercraft safety course, instructed by the U. S. Coast Guard.

Clifford agreed to go, and I came with him, so I could keep him company on the one hundred mile trip to Minneapolis. We both attended classes together, due to him encouraging me to also know how to operate the boat and be able to help when needed. Cliff was the one officially enrolled in the Coast Guard class and I was also allowed to attend. I absorbed most of the information.

During one class, the Coast Guard instructor told us the story of his best buddy, who had a fatal heart attack while piloting the boat. He said, "You know what happens next: the First Officer of the watercraft had better be knowledgeable enough to navigate the boat back to shore."

On the way home from that class, I told Cliff to count me out for any long boat trip, because I would never be able to get us back to shore. I would not know which direction I should be going. All the waterways look the same to me. I did not even know my directions on the ground and never would be able to navigate our boat in the right direction. Cliff said, "Don't worry, you will learn." I told Cliff, "No, I am not going down the Mississippi River with you."

In the next class, the instructor was teaching us about safety and fire hazards aboard watercraft. He said, "You know what happens when there is a major fire on board? You jump and swim." On the way home from that class, I told Cliff, "No, I'm not going down the Mississippi River with you because I would never jump off the boat to drown." Cliff said, "Honey, if we go, we would go together." And I said, "No, you can go by yourself, I am not going to go with you because I am too young to die." Cliff thought he still had plenty of time to convince me that going down the Mississippi River was safe.

Cliff continued to take the Lida Rose on shorter fishing trips, on which I occasionally also went along. On a week when the weather was forecast to be good, Cliff and I decided to go salmon fishing at Two Harbors Wisconsin. After a long drive from Minnesota to the western shore of Lake Michigan, we arrived on a day when the sun was shining and the sky looked great. While we sailed out to where the fishing was supposed to be good, the waters were calm. Cliff rigged up all the fishing lines. After a very short time, the clouds and the fog rolled in exceedingly fast and the water became extremely turbulent. Cliff had me take the controls and keep the boat on a certain course back to the marina while he pulled in all the lines.

This storm was so severe and that I could not see where any other boats might be. I was almost in a state of panic, but knew I had to stay calm and keep a careful watch for any other approaching boats. The visibility was zero and the turbulence heavy. I was scared and believe that Cliff was too, but he didn't admit that he was to me. I was ever so thankful when we did make it back to shore. I believe I constantly prayed and hoped God was watching over us. I was glad that it was the end of my fishing for that day.

At a later time, Cliff and I took a week's vacation with the Lida Rose in northern MN. Cliff had previously found a large marina to keep our boat for the summer in the town of Tower, Minnesota on a very large lake called Lake Vermilion.

Mail was delivered each day by boat. Cliff and I were lucky to be able to go on the mail route with the mailman, and it took about three hours to get all the mail delivered. It was fun and educational to find out that not all mail is delivered by land.

During that week, we were involved in another bad storm. Although we were docked in the marina, sleeping inside our boat, it felt to me that the wind was strong enough to tip over the boat.

At that time, the marina was owned by the city of Tower. Even though it was a beautiful marina, with many docking spaces, it was not doing all that well financially and the city wished to either sell it or at least replace the current management.

Cliff was interested in this opportunity, as it seemed challenging to him and would give us a paid summer getaway. He thought we should buy it. I was against buying the marina as the weather in this town was extremely frigid and the marina would be deserted during the winter season.

Cliff asked me how I would like to own this place? I immediately said, "No." Somehow, I convinced Cliff not to consider buying it, which I felt was a wise decision.

After my marriage with ended, Cliff did take his trip down the Mississippi with Robert Sterner, the brother of his good friend Don Sterner. Cliff told me that it was quite an experience, even though there we some difficulties.

The Sanders Friends Forever

Clifford knew Ivan (Mabel Sander's Son) nearly all his life and they both graduated from Little Falls High School together. I attended three class reunions with Cliff and knew many of his high school graduating classmates. Dorothy and Ivan married in 1949, just a few months before Cliff and I married. Ivan entered the U. S. Army in 1945 and Cliff enlisted in the Navy in the same year that they both graduated from high school.

Ivan and Dorothy devoted many years of service to the VFW Post #9073 in Randall, Minnesota, serving respectively as Commander and President of the Ladies Auxiliary. Cliff and I were members of that post for many years. On June 1, 1999, Ivan passed away at the age of seventy-two.

Dorothy, Ivan, Cliff and I traveled together many times in our motor homes to numerous places. One year we decided to travel through Plains, Georgia, to visit President Jimmy and Rosalynd Carter's hometown. Rosalyn had just written a memoir type book, titled <u>Lady from Plains.</u> It would be of historic value to stop in Plains and check out this town. Any presidential hometown should be a place to remember. We saw where President Carter's home was located, but it was hidden behind high fences and shut off from view. There was one old-fashioned drug store in town, was owned and operated by Rosalynd's cousin. She told us that she played with Rosalynd for years when they were young children and expressed a great deal of annoyance with her for never mentioning it in her book.

After Ivan Sanders died, Cliff and his wife Leone sent me the funeral program and a copy of the eulogy that Cliff delivered at Ivan's funeral. My son Richard helped Cliff to write this eulogy and I am including a part of it in honor of Ivan. In this part, Cliff tells the story of a fishing outing with Ivan that could have been a disaster.

"The most scary time with Ivan took place on a fishing trip to Lake Michigan in the 1980's. In early morning, we left the dock in Ivan's 16-foot open boat in fog. We figured the fog would lift as the sun came up. The visibility was less than five car lengths. I was a little concerned and asked Ivan if he had a compass. He said, "No problem." Ivan was piloting the boat and I suggested he keep the shore or other boats in sight at all time, so we wouldn't get lost. I was occupied with putting out our fishing lines and didn't notice that we had lost sight of the shore and any other boats. It was time to use Ivan's compass and the only problem was, it wouldn't point in any one direction. After a few minutes, it began raining, then storming with thunder and lightning. As I said, it was an open boat.

Based on my experience with storms on Lake Superior and as a Navy sailor on the Atlantic and Pacific Oceans, I knew we were in serious trouble and I immediately pulled in the fishing lines. Ivan snapped, "How are we going to catch any fish without any fishing lines in the water?" At this point, fishing was my least concern. That was the thing about Ivan. No matter what was happening, he was calm and completely fearless. A few minutes later, the boat engine quit because we were out of gas. Ivan said, "No problem, I have a can of gas on the boat." Ivan had previously drained the gas out of the motor home by using a cut off water hose that he found laying on the dock. He removed the rag, which was serving as the gas cap and began pouring the gas into the boat gas tank near the motor. I was very concerned about the heavy down pour of rain getting in the gas, which would keep the engine from restarting and even more concerned about both of us going up in a ball of flame, if lightning should happen to strike at the time. Being we were the highest thing in water, this was a very real possibility.

Before the motor started back up, we were able to faintly hear a foghorn and we now knew which direction to steer. But with a useless compass, we couldn't just set a heading and go. We had to keep turning off the motor to listen, regain our bearings, then turn it back on to again go the right direction. We finally sighted land, but it was in another city, six miles from where we started. With 60 miles of water and fog on one side and land on the other, we more wisely kept sight of the shore as we returned to our homeport. Trips with Ivan were most always an adventure."

Chasing The Beefalo

Although Cliff and I lived the later years of our marriage on a one hundred acre farm just north of Randall, MN, we did not actually do farming work, until we began raising Beefalo, a form of hybrid cattle, obtained by crossing a cow with a buffalo. For a time, Cliff was the president of the Beefalo Association in Minnesota. Beefalo meat is very lean, making it healthier than regular beef.

One bitter winter day, Cliff found a fresh beefalo calf that was born out in the field of our farm field. Because the mother cow did not want to nurse it, Cliff carried the baby calf into our basement and built a little home for it on some hay, and hand fed that baby calf hoping it would be okay. Days later it did die, but I will never forget having a real baby calf living in our basement.

On a day when the weather was extremely miserable, went to an auction with some neighbors, Betty and Rudy Anderson. I did not know where Cliff was, so could not tell him I would be gone and did not write a note because he usually was gone for long periods of time doing many things. The weather continued to get worse. By the time the auction was finally over and I arrived back at our farm, the gate to the farm, which was usually open was closed.

Immediately after opening the gate and driving in, I spotted all of our Beefalo in the front field where they did not belong. Cliff was on his motorbike trying to round up the beefalos along with the help of our dog, Toto. Cliff was not happy. He had been trying to get the beefalo back in their proper fences for hours. Because he additional help to herd them in and I was not at home to help, he was in a terrible mood. He was hurting badly because the cold damp weather made his knees even more painful than usual and he had been out in the field for hours without making any progress.

He promptly told me what to do. But first, I went to the garage to get a broom to hold in my hands for a weapon because of afraid of the beefalo. Between Cliff on the motorbike, our dog Toto and me, we started to round them up. My job was to bring up the rear. We had to be extremely careful that they went directly into the fenced yard and not to the small river on our property.

After nearly an hour, we finally rounded them all up and had them pointed towards their fences. I then must have spooked them in some way, because they all took off again and ran to the river. We had to round them up all over again and finally did get them into the fences.

This was one of the most miserable experiences in my life. Trying to get a 'city slicker' to round up cattle is a disaster waiting to happen. Cliff got over being angry with me, but I will never forget this story. Now, years later, I never have to chase cows and help fix fences again.

One bitter winter day, Cliff found a fresh beefalo calf that was born out in the field of our farm field. Because the mother cow did not want to nurse it, Cliff carried the baby calf into our basement and built a little home for it on some hay, and hand fed that baby calf hoping it would be okay. Days later it did die, but I will never forget having a real baby calf living in our basement.

Gambling Management

Cliff always wanted my help. It did not matter if we were at the office, at home, in the yard, or the pasture, fixing fence, chasing cows, or helping him fix something. We never seemed to stop working. I stopped working after I left the office, fixed supper, did the dishes and thought the rest of the evening should be mine. Being married seemed to be always filled with a constant state of activity.

Cliff told me, "You never want to go anywhere." His idea of taking me somewhere was going up north to one of the resorts that sold pull-tabs for the State of MN. Our time together was to count and pick up tickets. Cliff was the Gambling

Manager for the Lincoln Area Business Association.

When I was President of the Association, we needed a new Gambling Manager and I chose Cliff for that position. That job was enormous, because we had five resorts involved in selling pull-tabs for the State. Cliff had to choose the kinds of pull-tabs to buy. All of the winning tickets had to be saved, counted and stored for the State to audit, if they desired. Cliff had to collect the money from the gambling operations, record all payments and pay- ing these resorts a certain amount for having the legalized gambling in their resorts. He was also responsible for all reports to the State. This was a huge job and Cliff did it for about five years.

A Motor Home Story

We purchased our thirty-two foot long 'Landau' motor home in Ohio. In the middle of some very bad winter weather, Cliff and I traveled to Ohio in our half-ton Dodge pickup to Ohio to purchase it with the plan of towing our truck back on the trailer that Cliff had brought along. Except it turned out that the truck did not quite fit on the trailer in a way that made it possible to tow the truck back home. I ended up having to drive the truck while Cliff drove the motor home and the trailer. I was extremely scared, but had no choice in the matter and had to follow him and drive on the freeways through the city of Chicago. It was terrible for me.

We took many enjoyable trips with our various motor homes, traveling with friends or alone to many places and shared joyful times. We joined our close, longtime friends, Betty and Don Sterner most every year, going to Canada to fish for a week at a time. and had a great time. When Cliff was in the Navy, LT, JG Sterner was one of the officers that served along with Cliff.

As we were getting close to our 39th year of marriage, we were visiting the Sterner's and I mentioned we were approaching this anniversary and Cliff stated, "If we make it." I thought that was a 'standing joke'. But as it turned out, it was not a joke, 'We did not make it'. We worked all the time and our life together was one of practically all business operations, with little time for personal joys. The past memories never vanish from my mind. The three sons and five grandchildren we had together are still a constant tie to the time of our lives that we shared, even as we moved on in different directions.

Part IV
My Sons

My Oldest Son Jim

James was named after our best man, James P. Dugas, now deceased.

Jim was our first son born in the Portsmouth Naval Hospital in VA, and our total expenditure to bring him into the world was $6.75. The Navy paid the balance. My one-week length of stay in the hospital after having James was typical for 1952.

When we took Jim home, I was afraid of my tiny baby and being a new mother. After some time, it got a little better and I was becoming more relaxed with our son. We did not have disposable diapers in 1952, only real cotton ones that had to be rinsed in the toilet bowl when soiled, washed and hung on the clothesline to dry. We did not have a washer and dryer. Moms were the ones that took care of changing their baby's diaper. That was part of the job description of being a mother in the '50s. Fathers did not do that stuff. It was woman's work.

I grew into motherhood and two years later, little Jimmy had a brother named Richard and now he became 'the big brother'. Two years later, another little guy was on the way. Jim was now four and Cliff and I thought we had better tell Jim that our family was going to be larger because another new baby would be arriving.

Jim was not too interested in another little baby joining our family. He said, "We already have one brother and we do not need another baby. What we need is a dog. Can we get a dog instead of a new baby?" Whether or not we had Jim's approval, little Greg was born in 1956 and now Jim had two little brothers.

When Jim was nine years old, we lived for one year in Randall, Minnesota. At that time, Clifford was on Navy recruiting duty in Minneapolis and would drive the one hundred miles home on the weekends. I was working at Brunswick Boats in Little Falls, Minnesota as a secretary to the advertising manager, Sumner Young. Clifford's mother, Florence, often took care of our sons during the week.

One day, I brought another secretary home with me because we were going somewhere together that evening and wished to drive in one car. She was sitting on the sofa in the living room while waiting for me and kept looking at one of the walls. She finally asked, "Why are those posters on that wall?" When I looked at the wall she was asking about, I discovered all the 'MOST WANTED CRIMINALS IN OUR COUNTRY'. I did not know that Jim had stopped by the Post Office and had asked the Postmaster if he could have their old wanted posters. Jim then had put them up on the living room wall, which was the first time I had seen them. Very soon after, Jim's great posters had to be removed.

When Jim was in the 8th grade, he participated in wrestling and was one of the best wrestlers on the team. He enjoyed the sport. One day, the school called us because there was a huge fight in the schoolyard involving Jim and a few other boys. Many students gathered to watch this fight. The school official told us that if they could have sold tickets to it, they would have made money. We were asked to pick up our son from school and they thought he would be okay.

In order to punish Jim for his part in this big fight, Cliff and I decided he could no longer participate in wrestling. This was not a good decision on our part.

Jim was black and blue all over, but he told us the other guy was even worse. In the next few hours, he became very ill, his stomach hurt him more than he could endure and we took him to the hospital. He had severe pain that would not stop. After Jim was examined, the physician determined that it was his appendix and Jim needed to be operated on immediately. After the surgery, the hospital staff showed us what they had removed from Jim's body. They said it was the largest appendix they had ever removed from a boy his age. They also said that we brought Jim to the hospital just in time to avoid a burst appendix. Jim was very sick for a while, but recovered remarkably well and went back to school after two weeks. Jim's biggest concern while recovering was that being out of school for a whole two weeks after a fight might be hard on his reputation as a tough fighter.

He graduated from Little Falls High School in 1970, and shortly after graduation, enlisted in the U. S. Navy, staying for four and a half years and receiving an honorable discharge.

Over the next four years, he traveled extensively in around the United States and foreign countries including a one and a half year work assignment in the Philippians, working for a US military contractor. He also worked on a tuna boat during that time.

Jim then enlisted in the U. S. Army. While Jim served in South Korea as Staff Sergeant in the U. S.

Army, he had the opportunity to be Mrs. Cheney's driver while her husband, Dick Cheney, our former Secretary of Defense was attending a security conference. Jim told me that he was the only driver allowed to wear civilian clothes, because Mrs. Cheney had her own position within the first Bush Administration as head of the "Endowment for the Humanities." She had her own agenda during her stay in South Korea, aside from being the wife of Mr. Cheney.

Jim would pick her up at the hotel along with the security agent assigned to protect her. He drove the bulletproof Hyundai limousine through the streets of Seoul, Korea, sandwiched between Korean security vehicles and military aid vehicles.

They brought up the rear of the four-vehicle group. "We had to drive fast and furious through the crowded streets of Seoul, keeping within feet of the vehicle in front as a security precaution. I took my cues from the armed security agent in the front passenger seat," Jim said.

"We visited schools, some cultural sights and were able to go to the American Ambassador, Donald Gregg's residence, for lunch. The drivers stayed in their vehicles," Jim said.

At the end of the three day assignment, Jim asked her if his driving was okay? She replied, "You are a great, but kind of, crazy driver."

Jim told me that Mrs. Cheney was a gracious lady with a sense of humor and being her driver was one of the most interesting assignments he had while being stationed in Korea.

After completing twenty years of military service, he retired, and completed college with a BA Degree with honors at Fayetteville, NC.

He later joined the Peace Corps and went to Bulgaria. When Jim returned home, he decided to live in Lubbock, Texas and had a good job with the city as a City Inspector. He later returned to Fayetteville, NC and continues to travel. He has done volunteer work in Israel and traveled in Europe.

My Middle Son Richard

Both Cliff and I were extremely proud of Richard's musical accomplishments. Richard has been an excellent saxophone player since he was in grade school, due to many hours of practicing. He played saxophone in rock bands, since he was age thirteen. After high school, where he was elected president of his high school band for three years in a row, he attended St. Johns University at Collegeville, Minnesota and the College of St. Benedict in St. Joseph, Minnesota with a major in music performance.

Part of his training included a month of study in

Paris, France, where he and several other college saxophone students were able to study with a saxophone quartet that was led by the teacher of saxophone at the Paris Conservatory of Music.

During his junior year in college, Richard played a recital along with a fellow student who was an accomplished classical piano player. I was overwhelmed with joy as his performance was superb.

Another interest that Richard had from his early high school years was natural health. He mostly ate vegetarian foods and used to go into the woods and fields to gather wild plants and herbs that he ate and made into tea. After contracting a very serious case of mononucleosis while in college, he used these natural health methods to get better.

In the first years of his career, Richard supported his young family as an insurance agent and risk management consultant. Later, he taught insurance licensing and insurance and risk management continuing education classes.

In 1992, Richard began his training in alternative healthcare and later that year started his private practice. He has a successful fulltime practice in various forms of therapeutic massage and bodywork including Acupressure and Polarity Therapy. He is also a yoga instructor and author, writing articles and books focused on natural health. He formed a publishing company to publish his writings and also edited and published this book.

Richard is the father of three grown children from his first marriage...Elizabeth, Sarah and Grant. Cliff and I spent many happy times with our grandchildren while they were growing up. Cliff was a great granddaddy and I was a doting grandma.

After his first marriage ended in early 1992, Richard looked up his high school and college girlfriend, Bonnett Gustafson. They fell in love, and along with family members and close friends, Richard and Bonnett were married on December 9, 1995. Even though it was one of the coldest winter days of the year, there was warmth and celebration inside with a very unique 'Shambhala' Ceremony. His three children all had a part in the ceremony. Bonnett looked beautiful in her lovely dress, and Richard's tie matched his bride's dress.

One the back page of their wedding announcements, this translation by Stephen Mitchell of Psalm 1 was printed:

Psalm 1

"Blessed are the man and the woman who have grown beyond their greed and have put an end to their hatred and no longer nourish illusions.

But they delight in the way things are and keep their hearts open, day and night. They are like trees planted near flowing rivers, which bear fruit when they are ready. Their leaves will not fall or wither. Everything they do will succeed."

Bonnett has been a counselor for over 20 years, working with mentally ill and developmentally disabled adults in residential settings. Her work is extremely challenging and stressful, however it brings her great joy and satisfaction. She also is actively involved in their healthcare practice and she now devotes more of her work time to her new career in herbal and nutritional supplement consulting.

Through their work, they are involved with many friends and associates in their community. They take time to connect with their family members including me. Richard and Bonnett also enjoy music and the arts, outdoor leisure activities and travel. They live in St. Cloud, Minnesota along with their cockatiels and parakeet.

High School Stories
About My Son Greg

We frequently visited Cliff's folks on their farm when our sons were quite young and grandma would always have her delicious (hot out of the oven) baked bread. For me, the smell and taste of home-baked bread is the most wonderful food. Our sons never had home-baked bread unless we visited the grandparents. Greg loved grandma's bread and he asked her, "Grandma, will you teach me how to bake bread?"

I remember Greg making bread one time. At the time, Greg was a young teenager and we were living on our sales lot in our manufactured double wide home. Greg was getting the dough ready to let rise. When it was time for him to knead it, he took a run from the living room to the dining room to punch the dough down. I guess that was the fun part of making his bread.

I also remember, Gregory taking culinary arts in high school. He was extremely interested in this class. For his major project, he chose to make 'Baked Alaska', which is a complicated sponge cake with ice cream in the middle, which I would never attempt to make. That did not stop Greg. I believe his homework project came out great and he received an A. One of his classmates decided to make wine. I have no idea how the wine came out, but I heard he was one of the happiest students in Greg's class.

He called home when he was in college to find out how to make 'wild rice'? I told him I used Betty Crocker's recipe and I read him the ingredients. The next time Greg came home from college for a short break, I was missing my Betty Crocker cookbook and many cookbooks later Greg has become a great cook.

Greg used to come home from college when all his clothes were dirty. He hated doing laundry. Every mother loves to see her college son, but the huge bag of laundry was not as welcomed. I decided to make a deal with Greg. I would do his laundry and he would wash the floors. The deal was made and I was happy with the clean floors and Greg was happy with his clean laundry.

All of our sons worked for their dad and me in the family business. Cliff taught Greg how to transport seventy foot mobile homes around the mobile home sales lot and gave him lessons about hauling them on the highways. Greg was either eighteen or nineteen and had recently obtained a commercial driving license when Cliff sent Greg to the Dickman Homes factory in Spencer, Wisconsin to pick up a very heavy, seventy foot mobile home to bring back to our sales lot. It was about three hundred and fifty miles from our lot in Little Falls.

A seventy-foot of home added to a fifteen foot truck is an extremely long unit to pull on the highway for three hundred and fifty miles. At that time, there were many curves and small towns between the factory in WI and our lot. The first thing that went wrong involved a very sharp turn that was quite close to the factory. Greg did not quite make the turn and part of the mobile home got stuck in a ditch. After assistance from the a tractor that the factory used to move their mobile homes around their own preemies, the mobile home was removed from the ditch and Greg was again on his way.

A number of miles, Greg ran into road construction. Due to the size of the mobile home and tow truck, he had to stop and get out of the truck to move each of the orange cones that were in his way so he would have enough room to get past each small part of that construction zone. Then he went back to replace each cone again. It was a huge, pain in the neck job. A highway patrol officer happened to see him and stopped him and asked, "What are you doing, Sonny?" Greg showed him his driver's license and after that major job, he was on his way again.

It was getting dark and he was required to stop pulling the home before dark. He found a roadside motel where he could pull in his truck and mobile home to park for the night and checked into the motel. That night, someone tried to break into his room and Greg was afraid. He called home and talked with his dad, and said, "I quit." Cliff sweet-talked Greg into returning to the lot with the mobile home and he did. In my view, it was miserable experience for Greg and never to my knowledge he never pulled another mobile home from the factory to our lot.

When Greg was a student at Purdue, he did not have sufficient funds to buy Cliff and I a Christmas gift, and decided to make something for us. We had a dining room table that was hexagon shaped. He previously fixed my deceased mother's sewing machine by making a new part out of a paper clip. And took the measurements of the table and made a terrific tablecloth for his gift. I treasured and used that tablecloth for years until it literally wore out.

Greg Chandler Is My Name & Flying Is My Game

When Greg was fifteen, he headed for the Little Falls Airport to look at the planes. That's what his mother thought, when he asked to be dropped off there. When I returned from Little Falls to pick up

Greg, I was told he was with an instructor, flying. I thought to myself, "How nice they are to give Greg an airplane ride?" Little did I know, he was taking his first flying lesson, which he paid for himself. From that day on, Greg was becoming a pilot. He soloed on the day of his sixteenth birthday. He was also the youngest pilot to fly into the Motley MN airstrip for the breakfast, causing the local newspaper to write the story that follows. Clifford and I were very proud of Greg. He passed his solo flight test about the time 'Morey's Fish Market' had their annual 'Fly-In Breakfast'. Pilots along with their families and friends would fly in from everywhere. It was a time to enjoy an excellent free breakfast and share some fun time with other pilots.

Greg became a licensed Private Pilot at the age of seventee, and later, a licensed Commercial Pilot. He also had an Instructor's License. Greg graduated from Little Falls High School and was enrolled at Purdue University in the Flight Technology Program to become a licensed flight engineer.

He graduated from Purdue University and was on his way to Karachi, Pakistan. It is located somewhere in this world where the weather is warm, the sand is everywhere, and the food makes you sick. Greg became a First Officer after a short while, flying for Aero America. He flew the airplanes the U. S. Airlines would no longer fly because they were not in a great condition. Aero

America kept these worn out planes in somewhat flying condition and Greg flew for them until he became a pilot with National Airlines, as a First Officer.

National Airlines was in the process of being merged with Pan Am Airlines, and Greg was soon a First Officer with Pan Am for a number of years, until they were no longer in business. Greg was out of a job as were all of their pilots. Now Greg is a Captain with United Airlines and is flying an Airbus out of O'Hare Airport in Chicago, to numerous cities around the country.

In November 29, 1975, <u>Mary Arntzen</u>, Staff Writer for the <u>Little Falls Transcript</u>, wrote this story.

LITTLE FALLS MAN FLYING HIGH

If you were a student at Purdue University in Lafayette, IN, and you wanted to come home to Little Falls, MN for Thanksgiving, you would face a 13-hour drive. Unless, of course, you would take the route the crow flies. Then it would take about half that time. When Greg Chandler comes home to visit his parents, Cliff and Millie Chandler, in Little Falls, he selects the second alternative - he flies his own plane. His single-engine Luscombe

8E cruises at about 100 m.p.h. Moreover, Chandler says there is no traffic problem. During the six-hour flight, he usually sees only about three other planes.

He is now a student at Purdue, which is an approved aviation school. He started his flight instruction under Veiko Harala at the Little Falls Municipal Airport, and now he is working on a BS degree in professional pilot technology and a flight engineer's rating for a Boeing 707. He has the usual classes in math and English, but he also studies meteorology and aircraft electricity and listens to commercial pilot lectures. He said that much of his time is spent in the air practicing maneuvers in precision flying. He said, "The best part of the program is the hours spent in the air devoted to long-distance flying."

Chandler is also a member of the Purdue Flying Team, which competes with other university teams in spot landing contests. He said it is more than just competition with other teams. "It's competition with yourself. You always try to do it a little better," Chandler said. He just earned his commercial license, which enables him to fly for hire. In the spring he will get his instrument-rating license, which will allow him to fly through the clouds when there is a low ceiling and poor visibility. After that it will be more school and hours of experience until he can walk into the hiring office of a major commercial airlines and ask for a job. Chandler says, "He never had second thoughts about the career. "Flying is addicting. I don't know how I could live without it," he said.

The following is part of a story by __John Martin__ __Ward__*, Staff Writer for the Little Falls Transcript on July 19, 1977.*

YOUNG PILOT CLIMBING FAST, BOUND FOR "707" COCKPIT

Not everybody has the good fortune to be working at a job they think is fun, but it can happen. Greg Chandler, 20, is a case in point. He is a pilot, loves to fly and if his dreams materialize, he will someday work for a major commercial airline. "I don't know what to say when somebody asks me why I love flying." Chandler said. "I just say "Fly once and see for yourself." In a short flight over his home near Randall, Chandler told an intrigued reporter taking in an incredible view of the countryside. "Flying just offers a whole new perspective.

Chandler has been interested in flying since he was a boy and would ride along with his father, also a pilot. He has a list of pilot's licenses just about as long as your arm, and it will be a little longer when he graduates from Purdue University, Lafayette, IN, next spring. He will be graduating with a BS degree in Professional Pilot Technology. The training he gets now is the same as commercial airlines give their pilots. "The flight engineer is responsible for the preflight of the airplane as monitoring its systems of fuel, electrical, hydraulic, air-conditioning and preservation. The training is intense because the engineer is supposed to know how everything in the plane works and what to do if it doesn't. It's a big job," Chandler said.

Chandler works on a simulator at the University, which can create anything you don't want to happen in the air. After successful completion of their work at school, the students go to Dallas, Texas to take their flight test in a 707. "It is an expensive proposition at $1800," Chandler said. Even with all his training and licenses, landing a job for a major airline could be a tough chore, but Chandler is aware of that.

Chandler returned to Purdue University recently to begin summer school, but he said he intends to commute on weekends, at least until he can finish up the students he has now. He'll be flying his own plane, a 1948 Luscombe.

... ...

Greg Graduates from Purdue & Starts His Career

He graduated from Purdue University and was on his way to Karachi, Pakistan. It is located somewhere in this world where the weather is warm, the sand is everywhere, and the food makes you sick. Greg became a

Karachi Pakistan in 1978

First Officer after a short while, flying for Aero

America. He flew the airplanes the U. S. Airlines would no longer fly because they were not in a great condition. Aero America kept these worn out planes in somewhat flying condition and Greg flew for them until he became a pilot with National Airlines, as a First Officer.

National Airlines was in the process of being merged with Pan Am Airlines, and Greg was soon a

First Officer with Pan Am for a number of years, until they were no longer in business. Greg was out of a job as were all of their pilots. Now Greg is a Captain with United Airlines and is flying an Airbus out of O'Hare Airport in Chicago, to numerous cities around the country.

On February 17, 1979, part of <u>*Doris Simonett*</u>*, Transcript Columnist for the Daily Transcript of Little Falls, MN wrote this story. (She is the wife of John Simonett, who became a MN Supreme Court Judge).*

<u>COUNTY MAN FLYS SOME OUT OF TROUBLE</u>

Greg Chandler, son of Mr. and Mrs. Clifford Chandler of Cushing, has been involved in flying foreigners out of Iran since before the State Department announcement. Chandler, visiting his parents this week, spoke of weekly landings he made at Iran's Teheran International Airport from mid December to mid January. Chandler is a pilot for Aero-America, a Seattle, Washington based charter airline, and had been flying routes for Pakistani Airlines, which had leased service from Aero-America. The weekly flight to Iran went empty and picked up passengers waiting to leave the country taking them to Pakistan.

The 150-passenger craft was "absolutely full" each time, Chandler said. No Americans were among the passengers, but there were Japanese and other Far Easterners who had been employed in Iran and were leaving with their families. During December and January, Chandler said the formerly busy Iran airport was idle, heavily guarded around the perimeter. His was the only plane moving during his brief stops of a half-hour or less.

To expedite operations, Chandler's craft carried its own baggage handlers. The plane would stop on the taxiway, loading passengers as quickly as possible and keeping two engines running. "Flight scheduling was random due to breakdown of Tehran's communications systems." He continued, "I know less about the Iranian situation than do most Americans from their newspapers and televisions." He had little idea what it would be like in Tehran during the weekly pick-up. But because the airport was very well guarded, it probably was the safest place in the city, he said.

Chandler was sent back to the United States on furlough after the contract with Pakistani Airlines ended.

Greg's Family
Sherry, Dakota & Mathew

Sometime in 1979, Greg was flying a 727 for
Pan Am Airlines as the First Officer. Before the
flight from Los Angeles to Miami, Greg introduced
Cliff and I to the Captain. Shortly after, we boarded
the plane. They still had seats available in the first
class section, so Cliff and I were seated there. We
were flying without charge because we were
Greg's parents. During our flight, Sherry was the
flight attendant assigned to serve the first class
section. At that time, Pan Am was an enormous
company and every time Greg was scheduled to
fly, he flew with both a different Captain and
flight crew.

Before the flight, the Captain asked Greg, "Did
you ever have your parents aboard a flight where
you were flying the plane?" Greg said, "No." The
Captain told Greg, he wished he had the opportunity to do that aspect of his life over, because his
own Dad never got to fly as a passenger when he
was flying the plane.

Ordinarily, the Captain and the First Officer take
turns, each flying 'a leg' and it was the Captain's
turn to fly the leg from Los Angeles to Miami.
When the Captain asked Greg if he would like to

fly the plane back to Miami, Greg said, "Yes."

Sherry, a slender, tall, attractive black woman, came over to where we were seated, and asked, "Are you Mr. & Mrs. Chandler?" Cliff said, "Yes, we are." Sherry said, "The Captain thought you would like to know that your son is flying the plane." We were overjoyed to know this and thanked the flight attendant. We could not help from thinking that our son was flying this huge plane and we were both on 'cloud nine'.

It was ironic for the parents to meet the gal on the very same day that their son also met her. Greg and Sherry must have hit it off that day because they planned their schedules so they could take many more flights together. Soon they were seeing each other often, dating and developing a long-term relationship. Several years later they were married. Cliff and I knew they were living together, but initially did not know that they also were married.

In 1985, a Justice of Peace in Fort Lauderdale married Greg and Sherry. Sometime later, Cliff and I were visited them at their home in Miramar, Florida. That is when we were first told that they were already married.

[Editor's Note: What seems relevant about my brother Greg's love relationship and eventual marriage to Sherry and its impact on my parents, had to do with racial prejudice.

*We grew up hearing that racial prejudice was
wrong from both our Mom and Dad. In the
1960's, when my brothers and I were kids, we
interacted with black people on occasion. There
was a house painter named Jesse James, who was
one of the subcontractors my Mom's employer
hired to paint his apartment buildings. We would
see Jesse James from time to time and during one
week, he painted our house and we got to know
him quite well. He was a cool guy, and told my
brothers and me lots of interesting stories. A few
times, we also saw his wife, a white woman, as
well as their three kids.*

*They seemed like a very happy family to me,
and from that first hand experience, my brothers
and I formed the opinion that people who love
each other can have a happy life, despite strong
societal pressures against interracial marriage.*

*With that background, I was somewhat sur-
prised with my parent's initial reaction to Greg's
girlfriend, Sherry. In my opinion, it was low-level
prejudice. They said that they really liked Sherry,
"...but what would their friends think?" Over a
several year time period, their attitude completely
evolved. They said that they no longer cared what
their biased friends might think and I believe they
let go of all racial prejudice.]*

Years later, my association with Sherry has
grown to one of deep love and fondness. I feel joy
in having her in my life. I believe that Cliff,
Sherry's father in law, feels the same way.

Prior to adopting children, in 1986, Sherry and Greg bought a beautiful gray poodle, that they named Jessie, and in 1989, they bought another bigger poodle, so Jessie would have a playmate, that they named Julio. Sometime during the month of September 2002, Julio died and was buried on their property in Kingston, IL. The entire family misses him, including their other puddle, Jessie.

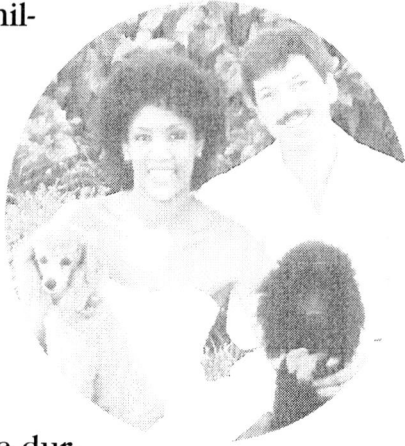

Their daughter Dakota was born on December 11, 1991 and she was adopted at birth. Her birth mother is 'White' deriving from Italian and Irish background, and her birth father is 'Black'.

On January 11, 1995, their son Matthew was adopted at birth and his 'birth mother' is White and his 'birth father' is of Native-American heredity.

Sherry, Greg, Dakota and Mathew all play the piano and take lessons. Greg's lessons are on hold while he completes major remodeling job of their home. Sherry's also has a hobby of writing lyrics for songs.

Greg continues to fix everything I may have problems with from my computer to toilets. When he is not fixing stuff for his mother, he continues to work on remodeling his home. In his limited relaxation time, he plays the piano, cooks and dedicates quality time to being a good dad and husband. The family is a loving happy one, and this grandma is thankful to be included in their lives.

Part V
Separation & Divorce

And Life Continues

During a period of twenty years, Cliff and I continued to operate our 'Ma and Pa' businesses. There was a fine line between being married and being business partners. Cliff and I were always friends and talked to each other. Our life was filled with both good and some bad times. He was a kind, gentle persuasive person wanting to be in control of everything. I allowed Cliff's controlling to continue and often felt like a puppet. We sold our small motel and I thought it would give us more time for other things besides work. That never happened.

After the motel was sold, Cliff said it was okay for me to start an insurance training school, along with our son, Richard. This school was to be located in Indiana. On the day we were to depart, Richard cancelled the trip. He felt that that a business operation in Indiana was simply too far away for him to be from his young children in Central Minnesota. I was extremely disappointed, because I was looking forward to participating in this new business venture with Richard.

It had been 20 years since I had lived in Minneapolis and it seemed to be the time for me to look at other ideas. I asked Richard to stop in St. Cloud to purchase a Minneapolis newspaper, as I wanted to look at the apartment rental ads. After checking a few places in Crystal and the Brooklyn Center area, I was amazed at how expensive the rental market was. The apartment I liked was on the second floor, clean and very empty. I did not know why I was renting this apartment.

Our family checkbook was with me as well as $1,000 in cash that I had saved. On that day, I rented the apartment in Brooklyn Center, signed a lease and cried. I wrote the check for the rent and the security deposit of $200. I had to sign a lease for one year. I did not even know why I was moving and tears came to my eyes while doing the paperwork.

The most difficult thing I had to do was to tell Cliff that I was moving to Minneapolis and wanted his help with the move. He could not believe this was happening and asked if I had given them any money for rent. I told him that I had written a check for the rent and the security deposit and signed a lease. Cliff was not happy about this decision made, but said he would help with the move. We did not even have a misunderstanding. We were too busy to argue often.

Cliff and I were always friends, as well as spouses and felt we got along as well or better than most of our friends. That did not mean our life was perfect. It was not. Cliff always got his way and was a great controller in his very kind, smooth and convincing manner. Our life was nearly a business partnership with all marriage benefits. This was the period of time when women were not equal partners in all decisions. The male was always the Commanding Officer, as they would say in the Navy. Cliff was a pleasant, kind, fair and an honest person, but always right.

Most of our forty-one years of marriage had been better than okay and other times they were not. There were painful times when I made Clifford very angry. He would stay that way for days, which hurt. It always left me with the question in my mind, "What was wrong with me and why am I not good enough?"

I asked Cliff for things necessary for my apartment including the spare 'white ash bedroom set' with a worn out box spring and mattress, the bookcase with my collectibles, some plants, an old oak mission desk and some living room furniture. I took cabinets filled with my doll collection, other collectibles. I took my clothes, some plants, a worn out ugly green sofa, a stuffed chair, a thirteen-inch colored TV and other miscellaneous stuff.

Cliff rented a truck and was assisted by the person that worked for him at the time, to help me move. I managed to round up pots and pans, some utensils, a small amount of dishes, and clothes. We were on our way to my new apartment with a fully loaded truck.

The truck was now full and it took Cliff, Richard, and the hired man the rest of the day to unload and set up my furniture. They were all tired and needed to return north. I thanked the hired man and gave Richard and Cliff each a hug and a kiss goodbye.

Clifford, Richard, and the helper worked all day setting up my apartment in June of 1988. It was a frightening experience to say the least. I was alone for the first time in my life for the past thirty-nine years. I was sixty years old. I had a thousand dollars I managed to save that Cliff did not know about. It was all the money I had to continue my new life and would need a job very soon. This was my new home and had to make this challenge work and extremely concerned.

I took the minimum amount of the things to set up housekeeping, which included breaking up the only six-piece set of Oneida flatware that Cliff and I ever had, which was given to us by our son, Greg. We both appreciated this set very much. I took four place settings and left Cliff with two pieces from each setting. He had other mixed utensils. I continually use these utensils and they remind me of the broken marriage. I managed to acquire one of Cliff's best filet knives and years later he discovered I had it. He said, "Hey, you have my good filet knife, the one I've been looking for!" I still have it and it is one of my best knives. I use it every day.

The truck was now full and it took Cliff, Richard, and the hired man the rest of the day to unload and set up my furniture. They were all tired and needed to return north. I thanked the hired man and gave Richard and Cliff each a hug and a kiss goodbye.

At age fifty-nine, after thirty-eight years of marriage, I bolted the door in my new quiet, lonely apartment. I covered the patio door with some sheets for privacy, realizing my life had changed forever and I was alone. The next day, I went shopping for food, being very careful not to overspend. Everything I needed to do for existing, as a single person seemed to involve a new step in being alone. Another page in my life had been turned.

I Settle Into My New Vocations

I needed a job if I were to live here. I had worked with Cliff from 1969 to 1988 in all of our businesses and had been out of the 'job market' for nearly twenty years. Every day, I put on my best skirt and blouse, white sandals, and panty-hose and went to the Brookdale Mall, as the apartment complex was located right across the highway from the mall. I filled out applications for employment with Sears and JCPenney. I took a part-time job with Jerry's New Market demonstrating various food products. It did not pay enough and was more interested in working full-time. I took another position doing telemarketing for cleaning furnaces and chimneys and was not happy doing that.

I finally received a call from JCPenney to come in for an interview and was hired to sell credit applications, which I did for seven years. I became the best selling associate of credit applications in the entire district, which included the States of MN, WI, ND, SD and IA. I earned a good salary because I was paid a bonus for each application, plus hourly wages. I ended up earning over $17,000 per year, for the first three years of my employment with JCPenney. That was excellent pay for that time. I enjoyed doing that work, and at times, I felt, I was almost my own boss working in the front of the store. In fact, I was the first sales associate, every customer saw as they entered.

My apartment was finally furnished quite nicely. Clifford had bought me a very nice used sofa from the Sterner's, daughter, Cindy, for $200.00 and I still have that sofa in my living room in Loves Park, IL. I won a recliner from JCPenney and gift certificates to buy my end tables and also purchased new draperies. Later I made several more purchases including new bedding, an oak dining room set and a curio cabinet. These were all purchased at JCPenney because of my employee's discount. Betty Sterner and I went shopping sometime in 1989 and I purchased a nineteen-inch television. My new furniture and apartment really pleased me.

There came a time when I decided that I wanted my insurance licenses reinstated and went to battle with the Insurance Commissioner, which involved a lot of paper work. After getting back my insurance licenses, I began working with an insurance agency in Brooklyn Center, and was given my own office. I only worked there two hours each morning, because of limited time and having my full-time job at JCPenney.

The Insurance Agency never gave me any established accounts and I had to get new customers myself. My package of insurance business was very small and not profitable for the Agency. After about a year and a half with them, I resigned, deciding to no longer write insurance and let my insurance licenses lapse forever.

It was the end of a very important part of my life because I had my licenses for nearly thirty years and those memories of business written, and not written, will always be part of my memories. Another page of my life had been turned.

A time came when the District Manager no longer wanted a desk taking up sales space in the front area of the store, because the area was more valuable for displaying clothing. My job was being eliminated and after some choices, I transferred to the shoe department until retiring from JCPenney.

Below is a poem I wrote about my JCPenney desk, written sometime in 1995.

THE DESK By: Millie Chandler

I'm just a desk and now I will be put to
rest,
I've lots of character and charm, full of fond
memories and many scratches.
My last seven years at the front of the store,
JCPenney at Brookdale, who could ask for
anything more?
Before I arrived at the front of the store,
I lived in the furniture department on the
second floor.
I do not remember how long I was there.

And so I was really getting old, but worth
my weight in gold.

Now I have to leave the store, no longer
appreciated here anymore.
This space I took up will now be filled with
merchandise.
New stuff for people to look at and buy.
Some of the customers will miss me and I
know why.

They used to stop and ask questions here,
Who can help me and is the restroom near?
I know I helped a lot.
I lived in this space for seven years.
The person that shared my life has shed a
few tears.

The memories, the customer caring, the
credit applications written at this desk, the
scratches, the nicks, even the hole someone
has kicked.
The worn out look with character of a per
fectly old desk, that has to go.
The store and the customers will miss me, I
know.
And it seems that "Millie" just cannot let
me go.

She is buying me and taking me home
With the memories of thousands of
JCPenney charge applications that were
written on me.

I will have a new life and be covered with books.
I'm just a desk, not being put to rest.
She is buying me and taking me home.
Now I will still belong and never be alone.
"I'm just a desk."

That desk is in my home office at
Loves Park and I use it every day.)

Cliff visited me at times. I was on my own ground now and he treated me with care. My visits to the farm were few, because I didn't like to make the long drive. All of our business checkbooks and business transactions remained with Cliff and I always worried whether he would get all the proper paper work done on time, such as the monthly sales tax. Cliff did not like me living in Minneapolis and several times asked, "Are you going to return to the farm?" My standard answer was, "I do not know, I need some more time."

The Divorce

Anyone's divorce could be the most difficult decision of a lifetime, and mine was exactly that. Many times during our married life, I thought there would be no such thing as a divorce and believed it would be a lasting marriage.

I never thought it was the most wonderful marriage anyone could have because I do not think there could be such 'wedded bliss'. I feel that marriage is something like stocks in the stock market. Sometimes the stocks are growing and getting better but sometimes things in our everyday lives cause indisputable problems that have to be solved. A marriage could not be a straight line, because in life there are some ups and downs. Without these ups and downs, it would be a boring life and we are not living in a perfect world.

After being married for over thirty-eight years, I moved to Minneapolis to live on my own. Part of me did not know why I had done that, but did.

The longer I lived on my own in my apartment, the more I began to find out new things about myself and discovered I could function as a single person. It was both strange and challenging and the question I asked myself was this: "Could I truly make it on my own at the age of sixty?"

Shortly after the separation, Cliff and I decided that we would not get a divorce at that time, to give us both more time to figure out what our future plans might be. Perhaps after a while, I might want to return back to the farm and remain married.

Sometime during the first Persian Gulf War, I had been thinking that I did not want to return to the farm and did not know if I ever would. I thought it was not fair to Cliff for me not to want to return to my former home. I needed to decide what I wanted to do with my life. Did I want to continue being his wife and go back? The answer seemed to be "No." I did not want to return to my past previous life. I decided to find an attorney and look into a divorce.

My plans were too frightening, so I remained quiet about them. Cliff had some idea that something was wrong. I finally told him and at that time, he was not happy. He did not want me to have an attorney and wanted us to work out our own divorce agreement. I would not allow my attorney to have the Sheriff's office serve the divorce papers on him. We made arrangements for Cliff to come to her office to be served.

This was a tough time. We sat down together in my kitchen with our books to work out the details. My attorney fees were reasonable. It took a lot of work to decide what we should each settle for because there were properties involved and we both wanted to be fair to each other.

Our court case was placed on the Hennepin Court docket, but it was going to be a long wait. Cliff decided that we should change all the paper work so the proceeding took place at the Morrison County Courthouse in Little Falls, Minnesota and my attorney then changed all the papers to the new location.

It took six months from the time of filing until the day of the divorce hearing. This period of time seemed to be the longest and most stressful six months of my life.

Cliff and I sat together in the newer section of the courthouse, while waiting for our case to come before the judge. While we waited, we talked and talked and talked about our entire life together.

I was divorced on April 2, 1991 in the Morrison County Court House at age sixty-three. Another page of my life had been turned. I was wearing a black suit, a white tailored blouse and a little red scarf. I called that suit my 'Divorce Suit' and wore it to work on the anniversary of my divorce for three more years.

Being married to Clifford was not an easy task for me. It was like a journey that seemed like a roller coaster ride with highs and lows. It was an adventure that created a great deal of activity and an enormous amount of hard work. It was the time that we shared taking us both through uncertain, constant periods called our married life. After forty-one years, on April 2, 1991, I was no longer the bride. The honeymoon was over. There was a divorce. My roses from my wedding were dead and pressed somewhere into my past life. My rolled-up oil-painted wedding portrait was lost forever, and that was the end of "The Wedding." Did this divorce happen because I felt I was not good enough?

On October 10, 1995, I wrote this poem for my Journalism class:

ONE DEAD ROSE

I have to say goodbye now.
My rose is dead.
Just a few days ago, it was so beautiful and alive.
Giving me pleasure and joy.
Some things give pleasure and joy just for a while.
And then they are gone forever.
I have to say goodbye now.
My rose is dead.

After the divorce, I was filled with many emotions that I could not altogether understand. My attorney suggested that I attend some self-help group meetings for people who were recently divorced. After several months, I decided to write out my thoughts about the marriage and divorce in a journal.

I wore my wedding rings for one year after my divorce, then removed them and put them away forever. At the time, I felt naked without my rings, but now going 'ring-less' longer bothers me.

One of the best things I liked about being single is that I do not have to hurry anymore. Life seemed to be better organized and I now do whatever I want to do. This is a good feeling. Life and the apartment seemed to be orderly and a new quality of peace came into my life that I had not known before.

Even though it has now been many years now since divorcing, there is not one day that goes by where I don't think of my former marriage. In my opinion, overall, it was a fairly good one and Cliff will always be part of my life memories as long as I live, because of our long marriage and because he is the father of my sons and the grandfather of my grandchildren. I no longer ask myself the question, "Was I not good enough?"

I now am not unhappy because of the divorce and am proud of my accomplishments in life since becoming single.

Return Of My Lost Wedding Portrait

In May of 2002, Cliff made a trip to Kingston, IL to bring Greg a part for his new tractor. Before he left Greg's home to return to Minnesota, he called me and said, "I brought you something." My reply was, "What did you bring me?"

Cliff said, "Remember that wedding portrait your sister Ruth painted of you in oil on canvas. I found it and thought you would like to have it."

I was astonished to hear that this painting had been found and I told Cliff I had just written about it in the book I was writing. Cliff said, "Maybe I should write a book too." I laughed and thanked him very much for bringing back this old painting that had been lost for over fifty years.

My oldest sister, Ruth, now in her eighties, painted this portrait from one of our wedding photos sometime in 1951. For some reason, I never had this painting framed. It remained rolled up and then seemed to be lost forever.

Greg and Sherry, (Greg's wife) each said in their own words, "Mom, we love it. Can we have it? We will display it somewhere in our house." Greg and Sherry had had it framed. On June 8, 2002, Sherry drove me to the dentist in Rockford and brought along the framed portrait for me.

I was astonished and overwhelmed of how

beautiful this painting was and the framing made the old portrait look spectacular. Greg and Sherry had the painting exquisitely framed in a very expensive gold painted frame. The colors in the portrait were vibrant and beautiful.

I found a home for it on my dining room wall. I have temporary custody of this portrait and then it will be given to Greg, Sherry and sister, Ruth had signed and dated it in 1950. What a treasure I have and it is too bad it took me over fifty years to appreciate it. A special thanks goes to the artist, my oldest sister, Ruth. I believe family members will cherish this beautiful portrait for many years.

Part VI
My New Life
As A Single Person

About Cars

What I know about cars is that when you get in them, they are supposed to go and be comfortable to drive. In 1988, when I first came to Minneapolis, I needed wheels.

Cliff and I owned a 1982 diesel Chevette that I first used. It was a nice little car, but touchy and only liked warm weather. I didn't even know how to put gas in the car, [*Editor's note: That was probably best that she didn't, as gas may have ruined the diesel motor]* because I never had to do it in Randall. Cliff always took care of that. When the weather got cooler, Cliff took back the diesel Chevette and brought me the 1972 Ford pickup to drive. The pickup was even harder for me to drive, because there wasn't power steering.

Next he bought me a 'junker' station wagon. I could not get the doors open when it was cold out and sometimes had to climb in the back tailgate to get into the car. I drove it for a while, but it was awful and I didn't like it.

Next, Cliff bought a gas powered Chevette down in FL and drove it back to Minnesota. A previous owner had modified the gas system, so it would run on the old leaded regular gas instead of the non-leaded gas that has been used for many years now. Something was very wrong with the car as I drove it. Oil went into the gas or oil pan and it broke down several times while on the highway while driving north from Brooklyn Center to Randall. It was too stressful to continue driving that car.

On my first day off, my friend Betty Sterner and I went shopping for cars. We went to three different dealers. The last place we went to was a large car dealership, 'Iten' Chevrolet. I took two cars out for test drives. One was a Ford Escort and the other a Chevrolet 1986 Cavalier. I liked the Cavalier best. It was clean and easy for me to drive. I made the deal and bought my first car.

I continued driving this car and so far it has been good. I had to learn how to put gas into a car and also to drive through a car wash, which scared me each time. Both things were major challenges for me to learn and accept because I had no other choice. If I was going to be on my own and drive, I certainly had to be able to take care of many new things in my life.

On October 16, 1992, I took my friend Shirley

Wunderlich shopping with me for a car. We traded my Cavalier in on a 1991 Dodge Spirit. We purchased the Dodge Spirit from the same person that both Shirley and her husband, Wundy, bought all their cars from. He gave me a good trade on the Cavalier. The Dodge Spirit had 23,000 miles on it and looked like a new car.

I'm still driving this car and like it. I promised myself that I would buy a new car when I graduated from college, but changed my mind because I don't like driving that much.

My Dodge has over 65,000 miles and I have no desire to get another vehicle because I only drive short distances in my area. My daughter-in-law, Sherry, or son, Greg keep my gas tank filled because I no longer want to put gas in my car. I hope to continue driving for a while longer, because when I no longer drive, I will become more dependent on others.

I do not like to drive in bad weather conditions. I have no sense of direction and am fearful of getting lost. I have been lost in my little area of Loves Park twice so far and that is enough times for me. My 1991 Dodge Spirit and I will be together for the next few years. It has a happy home in my two-car garage. A person I walk with told me, "Hang on to that car because it will be a collector's car in a few years." Someday, I would like to give it to my granddaughter, Dakota.

My Friend Shirley Wunderlich

When I met my coworker, Shirley, at JCPenney, she was working in 'ladies coats and suits'. Like me, she was a doll collector. She was also an excellent ice skater and took weekly skating lessons. At one time, she was part of a precision skating team that traveled to Europe to perform. She invited me to go skating with her, so I could watch. I never wanted to watch anything I could not participate in.

Although up until then, I had only done roller skating, I did go ice skating with her for a number of months and was getting pretty good, but I still missed my wheels. She knew some roller skaters, and she asked a several of them to contact me, and soon I was roller-skating again.

Shirley is still one of my closet friends. She working has worked at JCPenney in the 'Men's Casual' department for many years. Although, as of this writing, she is almost eighty years old, she still works part-time, ice-skates and does many interesting things with her friends and family.

Shirley's husband, 'Wundy' is also my friend. Years ago he made a bookcase for me years and also restored my beautiful mission desk where I am now working. He also made a special shelf for my 'Disney Globe' collection. I value their friendship. They helped me with bringing order to my new life.

The Dating Game–Arnie

It was difficult for me to be single again after forty-one years of marriage. I made a promise to myself to remove my wedding rings one full year after the divorce. On April 2, 1992, they were removed from my left ring finger and put away forever. It felt like I was removing the part of my past life that was no longer mine. It was now the time to get on with the rest of my life, including being single again.

I met Arnie while roller-skating. He was a nice looking man with a thick, dark, black head of hair, was friendly with all the gals and did some of the roller-skating dance steps. He also went to the senior dances almost every day. He seemed to know everyone and everyone seemed to know Arnie.

On October 10, 1992, I went out on my first date, if you can call it a date. My friend, Shirley, and I talked about it beforehand. I told her that I was going dancing with my friend Arnie. "You're going on a date?" she asked. I said, "No, it's not a date." She said, "If it's not a date, what is it?" I said, "I

eight dozen or more at a time, and I gave him half. He never paid for any of my expenses and was never asked to, which was my mistake. He ate one muffin for his lunch each day.

Diana Nilles, My Mall Walking Friend

While Arnie and I walked the mall, we both had the opportunity to meet Diana Nilles, a gal that became one of my best friends. Diana and I walked together for over ten years. We still keep in touch with each other. Diana was just a little older than my son, Jim. She was very pretty and Diana walked me through my divorce with Cliff and I walked her through her divorce with her husband, Mike, after a seventeen-year marriage. She invited me to her home numerous times for special events and I felt practically like a member of her family.

While Diana, Arnie, and I were walking one morning, Arnie got a brainstorm to play a trick on everyone at the VFW. It involved our good-looking friend, Diana. That upcoming weekend included 'April Fools Day'. Arnie asked Diana if she would help him with a trick on everyone. There was going to be a good band that night and he asked Diana to meet him at the VFW as his date. He thought that would make everyone wonder about how he could get such a 'young and pretty' gal to date him. She thought it would be fun and consented to go along with his plan.

I was no longer Arnie's girlfriend at that time and he did not want me to sit at their table. I wasn't about to miss that for anything, so I managed to invite another good dancer, I knew, to go to the VFW with me so we could watch the action that night. I wouldn't have missed this night for anything.

In the meantime, Diana had invited her sister-in-law to come to the VFW that night too, because she was going to play a trick on Arnie. I heard the plan in the ladies restroom and it was wild. Diana pretended not to know her sister-in-law. She was another pretty young gal, too, that also happened to be wearing a sexy dress for the occasion.

Everyone was astonished when Arnie walked in with Diana. No one knew her. The band was overwhelmed when she and Arnie were dancing together and he was overjoyed because he knew everyone was watching him, wondering whom this pretty gal was. They all wondered, how Arnie merited the privilege to even have her for a partner. He was not the best dancer in the world. After a while when Diana and he were out on the dance floor, her sister-in-law came in, unknown to everyone and she asked if she could cut in. Diana looked angry and played the part well. The other gal cut in and Diana walked off the floor like she was upset.

Arnie began to get the feeling that he was the greatest, most wonderful guy around for all those young chicks to dig him. The band and everyone at the VFW were buzzing and wondering, why Arnie? It was a fascinating evening and to this day, neither, Diana or I ever told him who the other gal was and he thought it was all his masculine charms that women seemed to admire. Diana and I shall share that terrific night of memories forever. He never found out the 'April Fool's joke was played on him, too.

My Friend Don N.

I could not sleep because I was remembering about my friend, Don. My friend Mary Newman had just sent me a short letter, enclosing an obituary about Don. He died on January 22, 2002 at the age of sixty-six in Hot Springs, Souh Dakota.

I have a technical line drawing that is framed that was created by Don displayed on the wall in my foyer. There is a small black box in the upper left portion that says "Hello in There." All the rest are lines and curves. It is one the neatest things I have. It will always represent my friend, Donald.

I have been feeling many emotions about Don and the impact he had on my life. It was during the spring months of 1994 when I first met Don at a senior dance I was attending with my friend, Arnie. I was age sixty-six at that time and Don was perhaps age fifty-eight.

I was dancing with Arnie, and looking around the dance floor to see who the other dancers were, when I spotted this younger looking guy with black horn-rimmed glasses, who looked scholastic. He was about 5'10", looked like a good dancer, and I asked myself, "What is that younger guy doing here at a senior dance?" I decided, someway or other, I was going to dance and talk with him. I had the opportunity, and took it.

From that day on, Don and I became good friends. He became a very important part of my life, turning it into new challenges, with opportunities that would change it forever.

We began to date and I became involved with activities such as meetings he attended with various professional people. They discussed the current topics of the day, which might have been social, political, or other issues of value. It was worthwhile and a growing time in my life to be involved with highly educated persons. I also attended some inventors meetings with Don. He considered himself an inventor. We participated in readers groups, where you read some of your writings. We attended my son, Richard's seminar in St. Cloud, Minnesota. Don and I assisted Richard with things at this seminar. Richard liked my friend, Don, and Don liked my son, Richard. They were both interested in eastern-arts and alternative health issues.

Don lived about two miles from my apartment in Brooklyn Center in a small white house in north Minneapolis. Don was an exceptionally clean person, as was his home. He loved music and taped many cassettes of music. He made me tapes of organ music and the music of Peggy Lee. Later I wrote a paper on one of her songs, "Is That All There Is?"

He was employed for a number of years with a large company in Sauk Rapids, MN as a technical writer and did most of his writing at home, in his loft. At one time, he was an English teacher. While going with Don, he was my own personal teacher because he seemed to be constantly teaching many different things to me, which improved my future life and I am thankful to him for that. The dictionary was his favorite book and he had me buy a good dictionary, which I used constantly during my college days and still use quite often.

During the early summer of 1994, Don and I planted four tomato plants in his yard that we shared. We visualized the abundance of tomatoes we were going to harvest. Our crop was limited, precious and small. We thought they were the tastiest tomatoes ever grown.

Don had a cat he dearly loved named 'Cat'. He was the proud owner of a 1988 white Toyota Camary with over 100,000 miles and he loved that car. He also played the organ and keyboards, which I loved. I would come over to his home, sit on his mother's 1900-stuffed sofa and listen to him play. He loved to have me listen and tried to teach me to play, but without success.

Don was the proud owner of two older motorcycles and often came over to help him work on them. One was a dirt bike and the other, a street bike. I became a bike rider with him and spent six months riding behind Don. The longest trip I made with him was one hundred miles.

One late afternoon while on the dirt bike, and on a trail, we hit a big hole and rolled the bike over, and I rolled with it. I was too dumb to know I supposed to get hurt and was in good physical condition because I was a walker. I just rolled off the bike on the ground, got up again, and was okay. The bike did not do as well and Don could not get the bike going again.

Don made me laugh. He had a weird sense of humor I enjoyed. He once told me, "I think I will keep you around because you laugh at all my jokes." I have never met any person that had the traits that he had. He loved to communicate, letting me know how important it was. He also motivated me to write in a journal as he did. We would read what we each wrote on the next day. He was also a health nut, and believed he could cure himself of any problems by alternative methods, without the assistance of a doctor.

He found out I did not know directions at all and insisted on teaching me east from west and north from south, while we were riding his bike. We would always go to the movies and everything with Donald was 'Dutch treat.' He never seemed to have any spare money and did not seem to care. I met some of his friends and they were very nice, interesting persons. We attended a 'blowing up of some old Federal buildings' and that was extremely interesting. We also went to a terrific 'Studebaker car show'.

Don insisted that we attend the 'Red Door Clinic', where we were both tested for the HIV Aids Virus because he would never become involved with any women unless they were tested for the virus. I was extremely scared to go. We became intimate . . . When I spent a night at his home, he would bring me breakfast in bed.

On one of the nights Don spent with me in my apartment, between sex and conversation, we decided to get up. It was about 2:00 a. m. We went into the living room, sat on the floor naked, eating bowls of cereal and talked. That was a first and last time in my life I ever had that experience. I saw this type of thing somewhere else, which seems appropriate - we didn't invent Bed & Breakfast -

we just brought it up to date.

After Don and I decided to no longer go together, his most important rule of dating became my rule, too. I later took a college class called 'Understanding Aids'. It was extremely valuable knowledge. Don had previously said, "Do you know what happens to a person that becomes affected with the Aids virus? They die." I became educated for the most important part of the dating game. Many seniors that are dating should be aware of the value of being safe rather than taking chances on what could be a dangerous or even fatal experience.

I wrote numerous college-papers for Gerontology classes that involved seniors and often stated how important it was for seniors to follow the rules of 'safe sex' like anyone else. Seniors are not exempt from any sex issues because they are older and the HIV Aids virus should be everyone's concern.

On August 10, 1994, one of our monthly discussion group meetings was being hosted by me, in my home. I decided my topic would be education, but I did not tell anyone, even Don. I wrote these words to introduce my topic of education at that meeting:

"I have been attending the Don N. Institute of Higher Education for the past four months and I learned a great deal. A few of the classes I attended at the Institute thus far were:"

Class I - Navigation. "It is a matter of survival to know where you are going." That was Don's favorite thing to tell me, as he taught me directions.

Class II - English: If you know a good deal of what is in the American Heritage Dictionary, you will graduate with a degree. So far, I had been making some progress. I had competed five % towards graduation.

Because the State of Minnesota does not recognize the Don N. Institute of Higher Education, I have decided to transfer to North Hennepin Community College as of September 19, 1994, and am now a 'College Student'.

While being friends with Don, I made this major decision. I became a student at NHCC in 1994 at age sixty-six because I wanted to learn more. While I did this on my own, I believe Don opened many doors and inspired me. He gave me the greatest gift of all, the desire to attend college and attain the experience of a higher education.

Over time, I was getting tired of being involved with Don, and he was having the same feelings. We both decided it was time to move on with our lives. Don and I remained friends. I knew he moved to South Dakota and was very sorry to hear of his death because he was an extremely important person in my life.

Roller Skating Days

I was roller skating again and having more fun than I could have ever imagined. For my sixty-fifth birthday, I had a short skating skirt made. What better present to give yourself when you are sixty-five, than a short, navy blue skating skirt, with tights. On the afternoon that it was completed I went to the skating rink. I cautiously skated out on the floor feeling somewhat naked. After getting over the fright and a few people telling me that my new skirt looked great, I seemed okay.

One of my skating friends, a big guy named Lincoln, who skated beautifully, waltzed with me. I began to feel great, and more secure, while having a wonderful time. When I got home, I put my skating skirt back on, along with my skates. I looked into the big wall mirror and was impressed. I was thinking, "The old gal looked pretty good."

On September 2, 1992, on a Wednesday night at about 10:00 P.M., I had a bad fall on the skating floor. I finally got up with help and could stand and then slowly started to skate again and seemed to be all right. I finished skating the session and a number of people told me that I would probably be black and blue. I never had one mark on me. The next morning however, I could not move and was suffering beyond words. A few years later, I had another serious fall on skates.

When starting college in 1994, I could no longer devote one night a week to roller-skating. It simply took too much homework and not enough time, I decided to discontinue skating. Now I have osteoporosis and have put my skates away forever, but not the memories of skating, fun and the many friendships that will always be with me. Another page of my life had been turned.

My Friend Mike

I first met Mike while attending an afternoon senior dance with my friend, Lucy. After dancing for about three hours, Lucy wanted to attend another dance at the VFW on 109th Street in Blaine, Minnesota, held every other Sunday. This VFW had the same band for many years, called the Jax Band, and they played country, waltzes, fox-trots, swing and some rock. When Lucy, me and a few others from the other dance arrived, it was packed. We found a place to sit and it looked like fun.

Mike asked me to dance and I said, "Okay." He was a good dancer and I enjoyed dancing with him. We danced the entire set. He asked me for my telephone number and I gave it to him on one of my deposit slips.

When Lucy found out what I did, she said, "You better get that slip back from him because you do not know who he is and your account number is on that slip." I thought about it and realized that was a dumb thing to do. I went to his table and asked for my slip back and tore off the bottom of the slip. Mike said, "I wasn't going to take too much out of your account." That was my first lesson to learn. Do not to trust people you do not know. I was innocent as any dumb person could be.

Mike called me soon and asked for a date. He was extremely nice and I was not used to a gentleman. I found Mike to be an ideal man friend. We dated often at first but because I was a student doing homework every free minute of time, decided to date only one day, either a Friday or a Saturday night each week. We continued dating for approximately two years. When I met Mike, he was in the process of dumping his last girl friend and of course I was happy because I liked him.

He took me out to dinner every single weekend and never had to share any expenses when I was with Mike. He paid for everything. He was the best dancer I ever met and I was on 'cloud nine' when I was dancing with him. If I could describe Mike in one word, I would say 'Charming'. He was retired from the Minnesota State Water Department. His wife had died of cancer five years before and I was divorced for five years as of 1996.

At the time I met Mike, he had just returned from a trip to Russia and was very excited about this trip. He told me that on the flight, he sat next to a woman from Estonia, a little independent country next to Russia. He enjoyed the conversation with her on the long trip back to the USA. She asked Mike for his address so she could send him a card from her country. He gave it to her. A few weeks after the trip, he received a card from her and was happy hearing from her and read it to me.

From then on, I seemed to be competing with her. Soon after we started dating, Mike let me know he was not interested in any commitments or anything further than dating. I told him I was okay with that because I was not looking for any commitment either. I was still adjusting to being single again after being married all my life.

Mike had a spacious home with a beautiful swimming pool and patio with a fenced in yard in New Brighton, Minnesota. He had a lovely flower garden with roses and other plants. He loved to garden and enjoyed grilling steaks along with a highball. He bought a special bottle of scotch, once he knew that I liked Scotch. I spent some afternoons on his patio deck doing homework or writing. I loved to write when I was with him. Mike seemed to motivate me to write.

I could not believe how happy I was when dating Mike. He was also a golfer and opened his home, to house two women golfers that were on one of the world golfing tours, which her held in Brooklyn Park, MN that year. The Golf Club asked for persons to open their homes for golfers to stay while they were on tour. They stayed in the spare bedroom on the lower level along with the family room and full bath. That was the walkout access to the patio and swimming pool. He saw very little of the golfers that were staying there.

One summer during the State Fair, he had to work in one of the political booths that prepared hot doughnuts, which was a way of raising funds for the Democratic Party. We went to the fair together and I was to amuse myself while Mike worked. I attended a music stage show. There was no charge for the show and every seat was taken.

Mike and I met for lunch. He had taken his camper because he could keep pop, drinks, and ice for breaks. That day, we ate junk for lunch as there is always tempting and interesting things to eat at a fair. We shared a big delicious onion. They cut it like a flower, dipped it in a batter and deep-fried it. Between the booze that Mike and I shared in his camper and that big onion, I became very sick later that day.

While Mike and I were dating, the gal he had met from Estonia was coming to Florida. She had a place to stay in Florida and asked him to join her and her friends. At first he did not know if he should go, then decided he would. She had a place where they golfed and dined and she seemed to be financially independent. He had a good time because when he returned, he told me he enjoyed the trip. Another time she invited him to New York and he joined her there. Finally, she invited him to visit her in Estonia and he took her up on that, too.

I continuously wrote Mike silly little things I thought of when I was with him. He kept every one, but before we broke up, I asked him if he still had them. He said, "Yes." I told him that I was going to write a book someday and wanted them back so I could do something creative with them. He returned them.

Then Mike invited the gal from Estonia to Minnesota and she came. During the entire time, Mike and I were dating, his Estonian friend was drifting in and out of his life. After his trip to Estonia, he broke up with her and with me. The last time I saw him, he was going with another lady.

In my heart, I cared for Mike more than he cared for me. Yes, I was heartbroken, when our two years of friendship ended. I was still a student and had other things to consider such as continuing my studies, with or without a broken heart. Life goes on and we face many disappointing things in our lifetime. Only my friend, Diana knew how hurt I was and it took me six months to get over Mike. I'm going to end with this poem I wrote, while going with Mike.

The Dancing Shoes

Now we lay down to rest
We danced tonight and did our best.
Just moving along to rock, country or
'A cuddly song'.

We were quite content and mostly upbeat.
We were filled with four happy feet.

We're very tired, but not singing the 'Blues'.
We're just what you would call
"The Dancing Shoes."

My Friend Phil

After being somewhat depressed for a while with my previous dating experience, I met Phil at one of the 109th VFW dances in Blaine, Minnesota. He seemed to be nice and was a good dancer. He had been married for about twelve years and was divorced for a number of years.

Phil was a man with high ideals. His dad had been a retired Lutheran minister, now deceased. Phil was a member of the Lutheran church, sang in the choir and also played in the bell choir.

On our first date, Phil brought me a collector doll named Margaret, to go with the other dolls he noticed that I had. Phil and I went dancing only once a week because I was in college. We often danced at the VFW Crystal Post #494, where I was a member of the Ladies Auxiliary or at the 109th

VFW and we both drank scotch and water. Phil was a good polka dancer and it was fun. We both enjoyed dancing and had a good time. Phil always paid for our drinks, but we never drank many. He had a cabin in northern Minnesota, approximately one hundred and forty miles from his home and he loved to spend much of his summers there.

At the time, I was taking a biology class at North Hennepin Community College. It was necessary for me to pass in order to get my Associate of Arts Degree and the class also required taking a lab along with the class, for five-credits. I never liked science in high school and only took general science because it was required. In high school, I had no idea that someday I would wish I had more scientific knowledge. For me, it took every bit of concentration, determination and memorization effort that I had. Often, this material was complicated for me and not understood.

Looking through a microscope was frightening and scary because never in my life had any experience with a microscope. I was hoping that someway I would be capable of learning and passing this difficult class. Phil agreed to come to the lab with me. He was knowledgeable about lab work and I needed his help. In addition to Phil's help, I also had a tutor. My biology problems continued, however. My life depended on passing this class because without passing, I would not graduate. I did pass with a C grade and this C was as good as any A. I was delighted and appreciated all Phil's generous help.

We went to Phil's cabin many times. It was peaceful and beautiful there. The lake was in his back yard. He loved it there. His friends from Bloomington, Minnesota, Duane and Lou, came up numerous of weekends and would bring food, as I did. Lou always brought enough to feed an army. We had great times attending auctions, fishing and eating too much. I was a camera nut when I was attending NHCC, because of needing to take photos due to my position as a staff writer for the college newspaper. Phil drove me all over the northern country and I took many interesting pictures.

Phil and I often went to a casino in Duluth. We also visited a special medical ship museum docked in the harbor on Lake Superior. That was a terrific experience. He would take me out to fish using oars because he did not have a motor on his boat. We would catch a few sunfish or crappies and as soon as we had enough for a meal, we would come into shore. Of coarse, Phil baited my hook and removed the fish, because I never did that. I enjoyed fishing, using my 404 'Zepco' fishing rod and always wore my life jacket, because it was the right thing to do and is the law.

Phil and I attended a number of his church pro

grams at his Lutheran Church, which had a very large congregation. He introduced me to the two ministers of his church and many of the members.

One summer weekend, I had a disastrous accident, slipping on the bath mat as I was stepping out of the deep, claw-foot, antique bathtub in Phil's cabin. After stepping out, the foot that was on the bath mat slipped and I seemed to hit every single fixture in the room. My head, neck, arms and back hit the toilet and the sink. I twisted all over the place and just lay on the floor unable to move. I cried for Phil to come quick. I knew I was severely hurt. When he came into the bathroom, I was lying on the floor in pain and told him not to touch me because I did not know if I could move. After a minute, I said, "Okay, now be very careful and let's see if I can stand up with your help." He gently helped me into an upright position and it seemed that I could stand. I said, "Now, let's see if I could walk with help." I did and walked slowly to the bed and he assisted me with lying down. Then called the local hospital and they told him to bring me in for examination. After helping me dress, he drove to the Moose Lake Hospital, where I was checked into emergency.

With probably lots of luck, being in excellent condition and because I was taking physical education classes at college, I did not break every bone in my body. They took x-rays and found no broken bones gave me some medication for pain and released me. They said if there were any problems to see my doctor. Phil drove me home and stayed with me that night to make sure I would be okay. A few days later, I had to go into the Unity Hospital in Anoka, Minnesota because I had severe pains in my stomach. I was kept overnight for tests. That was on a weekend and did not want to stay in the hospital so they released me.

I had to get back to work and school regardless of the fact that I was black and blue all over. It looked like I was in an abusive relationship of some sort and was questioned about it. I assured everyone, it was an out of the ordinary accident. The college term was soon ending and I had to complete all my classes or fail. The physical education class required that I exercise for one and a half hour sessions, three times a week to get an A. My instructors were told I could not use the different machines required for each class, so they said, I would have to walk instead. These remaining classes were spent walking around the gym for the required time and I firmly believe it helped me with a faster recovery. That was the worst fall I ever had. No wonder I have osteoporosis now. Mall walking makes me feel healthier and stronger and I hope to remain active for some time.

Phil took my friends, Shirley and Mary and me to my graduation from Metropolitan State

University, even though there were terrible winter storms that night. There were highway warnings not to drive during this storm. The visibility was zero and newscasters were stating that driving conditions were unsafe. The highway was nearly deserted, which was lucky for us.

Phil's car started spinning out of control and it was terrifying. It was a good thing there weren't any other cars coming toward us or we would have all been killed. Phil's car got dented in the rear, but it wasn't nearly as bad as it could've been. My friends and I will never forget that trip and we were all thanking God because it was probably a miracle that none of us were seriously injured or killed on that stormy graduation night.

Phil attended both of my college graduation from NHCC and MSU in 1997 and again in January of 2000. After approximately two years of dating Phil, I seemed to lose interest in dating. We remained friends and he called me every few months for a few years.

When I left Minnesota, I never got a chance to let him know I was moving from the state. Phil now has my new address and email address so we can keep in touch because he is my friend.

My Friend Ray

Quite some time ago I was working part-time with Midwest Area Insurance Agency as an insurance agent while employed full-time at JCPenney. Ray Anderson was also an agent at this agency. He had retired from Northwest Bank when Wells Fargo bought the bank and had been an Assistant Vice-President, in charge of the Insurance Department. He was not ready for retirement and his office at Midwest Area Insurance was located right across from my office.

Many of Ray's customers from his former position continued to do business with him in his new insurance agency. I did not have sufficient insurance leads and had to work for every piece of new insurance business. I only could devote a few hours per day, three times per week to insurance sales. Ray was always busy on the telephone, getting new business and doing a great job. At times, I would go to his office to visit and learn new insurance ideas that would benefit my sales.

He was a gentleman, handsome, and married. One time he was taking his mother shopping at JCPenney and because my desk was located at the front door, they stopped by to say hello and he introduced me to his mother. Another time, he was in the store with his wife, and again stopped by to say hello and he introduced her to me.

I continued to work at the agency for over a year.
The company was paying enormous premiums for
'Errors and Omissions Insurance' for each person
writing business for them. Because my book of
business was not sufficient for me to remain with
them, I resigned.

One day, Ray came into the Shoe Department
and told me that his wife divorced him after forty-
two years of marriage. He knew that I was
divorced too, after a long marriage. He was
extremely unhappy about the divorce. Ray and I
then started to date. He was a 'health nut' and
loved walking outdoors. He would pick me up on
weekends to drive to Lake Calhoun and other area
lakes and then would walk as much as three miles
around these beautiful lakes. That summer, I
walked around all the lakes in the Minneapolis
and St. Paul area. He always took me to lunch after
walking. We also went to a few dances and out for
dinner. His town home was located about a mile
away from mine.

The Insurance Agency we both had worked for
was now closed and Ray then worked part-time
with another agency. He was a devout golfer and
involved with his church. He went to the gym
everyday and also did volunteer work there. He
was a handsome, distinguished man with white
hair and I enjoyed our friendship. He graduated
from college right after he completed a tour of

duty in the military.

I was still a student while we were dating. Ray drove me to the St. Paul Campus of Metropolitan State University to attend orientation classes and waited for my day to end to take me home. He also drove to Randall, Minnesota with me and went along for the interview I had with Mabel Sanders, who was one hundred years old. Ray took the picture of Mabel and me that was published with the story I wrote. This was the first news story I ever had published and I was very proud. It was published in the 'Morrison County Record'.

That same day, Ray and I visited with Cliff's Aunt Gladys. She was delighted to have the visit. Gladys died in her mid nineties after quite a few years of poor health. I communicated with Gladys every Christmas season. One of her daughter's, Joyce, is exactly the same age as I am. We were both born on the same day and year.

Ray left Minnesota every winter to go to Texas with some other golfers, staying the entire winter season. He spent both winters and summers golfing. Ray and I did not resume dating after he returned and that was the end of the dating game for me. Another page in my life has been turned.

Back To School

I started college at North Hennepin Community College in Brooklyn Park, Minnesota at age sixty-seven as a first year student. I felt an enormous need to attend college because I never had the opportunity before. This was the most difficult and rewarding decision I ever made.

The first night of class was on September 19th, 1994 and I was extremely scared of becoming a student and being an older person. There were many obstacles to conquer but I managed to survive them. The next few years of my life were constantly challenging ones. I kept asking myself; "Can I do this?" "Will I do okay?" "Can I succeed as well as much younger students?"

I constantly wondered if I would pass all my required classes. It was tough. I attended summer school every year and never stopped doing homework. It took me two and a half years to achieve my Associate Arts Degree and an additional one and half years to graduate from Metropolitan State University. On the 17th day of December 1998, at the age of seventy-one, I received my Bachelor of Arts Degree in Human Services. I was the proudest grandma and oldest student enrolled at both colleges.

On March 15,1995, this bold comment in larger letters appeared on the front page of our college newspaper, <u>THE NORTH STAR</u>. "Going back to school can be a daunting task, just ask Millie Chandler. She returns to school after a rich and colorful life to find that you can never stop learning. Listed below is that story: *[Editors Note: The following story appears as it was published in The North Star college newspaper.]*

<u>Is That All There Is?</u>

It all started during the summer of 1994. I was speed walking at the Brookdale Mall. It was sometime between Monday and Friday, at 8:30A.M when my daily routine for walking began for six times around the mall in one hour before work. That was a little over four miles and it made me feel like I'd accomplished something for me. I felt healthier, happier, and could probably eat more because I've used some energy. While walking, I did some thinking about anything and everything.

During the summer of 1994, I also had a special friend, Don N. He was not only my friend, but also more like my teacher. In fact, he had been a teacher, but was now a technical writer. He believed in communication and said, "Everything we do everyday when there is more than one person involved is communicate." I enjoyed communicating and learning from everyone. I soon discovered how much there was to learn, and to use your mind was great.

Back to my mall walking…I kept the thought of wanting to go to college and again let the thought drift away, and went about my usual routine business of working, walking, skating, dancing, TV watching, reading, and just normal living. There's an old song, Peggy Lee made famous, "IS THAT ALL THERE IS?"

Sometime later, while mall walking, again, I thought, 'Yes, I do want to continue my education'. I decided to check with personnel at JCPenney to see if there were any scholarships available for their employees to attend college and was told that employee's children would qualify, but not the employee. Well, that took care of that. Still, it bothered me and thought I should check out a college and see what it is all about. It had been so long since I had been in school because I graduated high school in 1946, married in 1949, had three sons, was married for 41 years, had four grandchildren, and one divorce, I thought to myself, "IS THAT ALL THERE IS?"

One summer day, on my day off work, I drove to North Hennepin Community College, to see what I was supposed to do in checking out a college. I was a little scared. I managed to find the building I was supposed to be and met with the counselor.

I thought everyone would be wondering, "What is this older person doing here?" No such luck, no one cared. The counselor answered some of my questions. I told him, I thought I would be interested in writing and speaking. He brought me a blue sheet of paper with the requirements for an Associate of Arts Degree. I left the college feeling a little smarter. At least I knew where the college was and where to find the counselor.

I had the college schedule and their manual. Now I can really find out what it is all about. My next step was to make an appointment with the counselor at Metropolitan State University. She was helpful, too. I put together my past business experiences as requested. She suggested I put in for some competency programs and then I could get some extra credits. It was almost time for college to begin, and I had to make some major decisions. Would I really be going to college, and which college should I attend? I decided it would be North Hennepin Community College.

Since I was a first generation student and it has been many years since I had been in school, I qualified for the "Alis Grant." I chose English 111 for my subject, enrolled in PL 101 and became a college student. In all my years of working, I have never heard so many complicated words in my entire life. I thought to myself, why can't they just speak English here and not have to make it so complicated. My first quarter, especially English was extremely difficult and soon learned that is what college is all about.

Now I am in my second quarter and not scared any more. A few new words have been learned and much more every single day especially what it is to do homework, and more homework. It never stops. I hope I am getting smarter. Whenever something new is learned not known before, I feel like I am accomplishing something with my life.

Some of my friends thought 'I was off my rocker' when I decided to go to college. They said, "What do you want to be when you grow up?" Maybe the answer is to become smarter.

I have done a lot of things in my life. Some of them were being a wife, a mother, a grandmother, a student pilot, a secretary, an office manager, licensed with Securities to sell mutual funds for over 15 years, licensed to sell Life and Casualty Insurance for many years, owned and operated a Manufactured Homes Sales Lot. We owned two mobile home parks, one small motel, lived on a hundred-acre farm and we had 40 head of 'Beefalo' and one ugly buffalo.

We had an air- strip on our farm and an air-plane, a boat, and a Motor Home. We never stopped working. We also owned an Insurance Agency, then a Satellite and Video Store. You name it, we had it or did it, and it seemed like just about everything.

In 1988, I moved to Minneapolis and went to work for JCPenney, and also for Midwest Area Insurance as a part-time Insurance Agent. I roller skated every week, and danced, and worked and worked. I went on with my life thinking, "IS THAT ALL THERE IS?"

There are many things in my life I have not done. I have an enormous desire to complete my AA Degree and go on to achieve my BA Degree. Yes, I am in a hurry. It is not easy. I have to work extremely hard to obtain good grades. I am very excited about attending college, and many times, it is the most difficult task I have endeavored.

Learning is wonderful, and I no longer have time to think about Peggy Lee's song, "IS THAT ALL THERE IS?" I'm just another college student, and my name is Millie.

(Peggy Lee has died since I originally wrote this and I am delighted, one of her songs influenced me enormously to use it for this paper.)

July 10th, 1995-Writing Workshop-English 196

[Editor's Note: The following story appears in its original unedited form.]

Long ago, when I attended school, algebra was

not required and our math classes were called Arithmetic. All I knew about algebra was 'Let X = something or other'. Most students seemed to be comfortable with algebra because they took it in high school. I had many problems because of not having the necessary background. Algebra was a required subject in order to obtain an AA Degree and I enrolled in a Summer School Class, which requires learning more in a shorter period of time.

I was heading for a nervous breakdown. The class was on chapter 5 and I was on chapter 3, and could not keep up. The first night we had to do 69 pages of the hardest problems a new algebra student could imagine. I wouldn't mind doing the major homework assignment if I understood what it was about. It became extremely difficult. I went to the library and checked out the videos to study Chapter 1 and 2. I visited the Math Learning Center twice for much needed assistance and hired a tutor that did not help either when he failed to show up.

My world was falling apart and life had become an algebraic challenge. Big test number 3 was approaching. All the new terminology was getting to me. There was so much to know, and I wasn't getting it. However, I knew I needed it to obtain my AA Degree. My algebra workbook became part of my dining room table. I began on page 1 again to see if I missed something.

My long lost tutor, I hired two weeks ago, to

teach me algebra, called. He wanted to know if I wanted an algebra lesson. I really didn't but good tutors are hard to find when you need them, so I said, "Okay." Forty minutes later, he arrived. Although I no longer was taking algebra, the little bit of knowledge and my expensive workbook are valuable assets from my college days.

I had to tackle Biology, Chemistry and Lab if I was going to get my AA Degree. This class was another difficult classes next to algebra. I studied and studied and had a tutor every week. Through many hours of study and some prayers I passed this class. I ended up with the best 'C' anyone could every hope for and achieve. That 'C' was better than any 'A' I could have obtained and was overwhelmed with joy and successfully graduated from NHCC in 1997.

November 25th, 1995, published in <u>THE NORTHSTAR</u>
[Editor's Note: The following story appears in its original published form.]

<u>BEING ROBBED AND ROUGHED UP</u>
I'm Very Angry and Why Should It Happen?

What does it feel like to be knocked down and

dragged; have your purse stolen and the next day,
you find your car was also stolen? At first I was
too surprised to be scared. It all happened so fast.
The time was 12:15A.M. Saturday on October
21,1995. The place was Brooklyn Center, the parking area where I have lived for nearly eight years
and have never been afraid nor thought this apartment complex was anything but a safe place. On
that night, I was proved wrong. It was the end of a
terrific evening, a date with my friend, Mike, of
dining, and dancing and we were on the way back
to my home. After a week of work, school and an
enormous amount of homework, a night out was
great. However, this one turned out to be a disaster

The thugs pinned Mike up against the first car
in the parking lot and held something that felt
cold to Mike, against his neck. It could have been
a gun. They said they wanted the keys. Mike said
something about, "Please guys, don't be that way." I
was right there to see if I could be of some help. I
was knocked to the ground and dragged across
the parking lot. My thoughts were - What should I
do? Do I scream or kick or cry? Thinking they're
three big Afro-American guys and only two of us, I
decided to remain quiet and I was too scared to
think clearly besides. My purse slipped from my
shoulder. One of them picked it up and all three
guys ran. They probably thought we were married
and when they had my purse, they had the keys

to Mike's car. They never searched Mike or even took his billfold. They wanted the keys to the car and they had my purse.

When they ran, we opened the security door, then my apartment door and called 911. After that call, the next one I made was to my Visa card company to cancel my stolen card. The Brooklyn Center Police Officers arrived shortly. We were told that someone just before my call had reported three suspicious looking men to 911. Information was taken from both Mike and me. So far, all that was taken was my purse. In my purse was my billfold, which was also a key chain with two keys on it. One key was my apartment door key and the other the key to my car. I also had my safe deposit key in my purse. It was not supposed to be there, but I did not take it out of my purse the last time I went to the bank. I had some money and my little black calendar book with my entire life history written in it. My driver's license, checkbook, social security card and other important documents were in my purse.

The police officers said they would look around for my purse in case they dumped it in the trash or someplace close by. After they left, Mike and I started to talk about what happened. My good leather coat was ruined from being dragged on the parking lot with me in it. Perhaps, it saved me from getting seriously injured. We talked about what we could have done, what we did not do, and tried to reason everything out. We decided that we were lucky we were not stabbed or shot, or really harmed more than we were. It was not over yet. The next morning my car was gone. I called 911 again and the Police Officer from the Auto Theft Division came over to get the particulars on my car. I was still extremely upset and angry.

I had to go to the Rental Office and request a change of locks on the apartment door. Next to the bank to close my checking account to start a new one. Then call both the Auto & Home Owner Claims of my insurance to let them know both my purse and car had been stolen.

"No Wheels" is very difficult when a car is needed to attend school. I could walk to work because I lived across the highway. When I wanted to rent a car, they would not allow me to do so because I did not have my driver's license. The Vehicle Division did not open on Monday's, so had to wait until Tuesday to get my driver's license renewed and have someone drive me there. Then the next day, I stopped to rent a car and needed a $500 security deposit to do that and a valid credit card. The stress and anger would not leave me. It was so bad the first day, I could not work so I lost an important day of work because I was too upset to sell shoes.

My car was gone for two weeks and thought I was never going to get it back. Thursday evening, around 11pm, the Brooklyn Center Police Department called me and said they found my car and had brought it to the crime lab and dusted it for fingerprints, and arranged to see me at work to pick out suspects from photos. I was not positive, but picked the ones I thought they were.

They picked me up to get my car and had to pay the cost of $113 for the impounding fee and sign the release and they took me to my car. It was very cold with bitter winds that night. The gas tank was on empty, and headed to the gas station. The rental car was returned costing $347 to drive 69 miles. Then have the locks changed in my car and the mechanical work checked to restore my car to the condition prior to the theft. I still had to have the safe deposit key replaced at a downtown location and the authorization from bank cost was $15 to have that key replaced.

Things like this should not happen. All the work involved is time consuming and troublesome. Others hear about something like this happening, but when it happened to me, then the situation became real. I had to be very thankful that we did not get hurt. I'm now more aware and cautious of my surroundings and shine the lights around the area before leaving my vehicle. I'm no longer as confident as I was about not being afraid. I guess it is okay for me to be angry because being angry is much better than being hurt or dead. Yes, this is the real world and sometimes it is not great.

On July 13th, 1998 for History #310 – History at the Movies, I wrote about <u>Bonnie & Clyde</u> & John Steinbeck's novel, <u>The Grapes of Wrath</u> and <u>Easy Rider</u> and had to compare them for similarities. The movie <u>Bonnie and Clyde</u> featured excitement with glamour, profanity and brutality. The main actors were Clyde Barrow (Warren Beatty) and Bonnie Parker (Faye Dunaway)

[Editor's Note: The following story appears in its original unedited form.]

Bonnie and Clyde

<u>Bonnie and Clyde</u> was it a movie about their notorious Barrow robberies during the Great Depression of the 1930s. It was a movie about a period of history being brought up to date with a mixture of past history, social issues and women's liberation, and a flavor of what our 1967 audiences would relate to. In order to make this movie a success, Arthur Penn, Director and his staff, twisted some fact with fiction to bring the new audiences into the past with perhaps some modern and up-to-date flare in telling the story.

According to Robert Toplin, author of <u>History by Hollywood</u>, this movie produced action from the

English songwriters and they produced the "Ballad of Bonnie and Clyde," a tune that climbed to first place on the British charts. The clothing industry was cashing in on new clothing designs for the United States as well as European markets.

Bonnie and Clyde created excitement in the fashion industry. Bonnie was beautiful as well as charming and daring to take on the world with Clyde. He introduced himself to Bonnie after she yelled at him for attempting to steal her mother's car. He told her, with a big handsome smile, "My name is Clyde Barrow and I just got out of state prison for robbery." Then he asked if she would like to see his gun? Bonnie was impressed and that was the beginning of their adventures of Bonnie and Clyde.

In the 1930s, when the banks were repossessing property because lack of funds to pay taxes or the mortgage payments. The people were put off their land and forced to leave. The banks and law enforcement were the ones with power and the poor people and farmers had to leave their homes. Yes, Bonnie and Clyde and the Barrow Gang were heroes to the poor people of the Great Depression of the 1930s. In the movie, Bonnie and Clyde had class, style and glamour, mixed with profanity and brutality, excitement and romance. It was everything a movie audience would appreciate. Bonnie Parker loved to write and near the end of the movie, she reads her poem to Clyde:

("Someday they'll go down together/ They'll bury them side by side/ To a few it'll be grief/ To the Law a relief/ But it's death to Bonnie and Clyde.") After Bonnie read this poem, Clyde finally became the lover she was longing for. It was the 'icing on the cake' for movie fans always love romance.

John Steinbeck's novel of <u>The Grapes of Wrath</u> tells a simple, depressing story of the Joad share-cropper family, living in the Dust Bowl during the Great Depression of the 1930s. This true story is about how life was during this period of time. It was made into a film casting Tom Joad, (Henry Fonda) and Ma Joad, (Jane Darwell). The Joads' home as well as the other sharecroppers' homes and land were going to be plowed over and turned into something called 'progress'.

The law enforcement and bankers were forcing all the sharecroppers off their land. They were given one day to vacate their property and every-thing remaining the next day would be plowed over. The lack of rain and years of continuous winds, blowing the entire top soil away and turned the land barren. It was the cause of near starvation and many deaths. Their most precious thing they had in life was the land where their fathers and all their children were born and it was supposed to belong to them forever. Being forced off and watching heavy machines bulldoze their homes to the ground was devastating. Joad return-ing home from prison, looking for his family found they moved west to stay with other members and joins them the next day and they are moving.

They had a flyer stating there was work for 800 people out west, picking peaches and good pay, giving them hope. They loaded their possessions and extended family, including Grampa, Grandma, pregnant daughter, the new husband, children, aunt and uncle, and a 'has-been' preacher whom Joad met the day before and invited him to come along since he did not have any other place to go. They were loaded, ready to move west in the broken down truck just purchased for $75. They had $200 for the trip less the cost of the truck. It was all the money they had and needed it to last until they had work. Grampa did not want to leave home. He said he would rather die on his land where all the other members of his family died. They decided to pull a fast one on Grampa, got him drunk, and loaded him into the truck. He soon died. They buried him, asking the preacher to say a prayer and then moved on. Ma Joad was the strongest, most sensible, determined and caring person of the family, continuing to keep the family's spirit, hope and strength together. Grandma Joad died next. The Joad Family was a story about one family that represented thousands of 'Okies' from the west and south forced off their land.

It was a story of sharecropper' families moving west to find work and keep their families from starving, stopping time to time at terrible transient camps. Children, mothers, older persons, all trying to stay alive and the crooks trying to make an extra buck off of these poor people by not paying them enough to stay alive. The transient camps, guards, and temporary housing were shameful because the 'Oakies' were treated like dirt. One of the happiest times is when the Joad family arrived at a federally run camp created by the Farm Security Administration for migrants. It was part of President Roosevelt's 'New Deal' and was a utopian to the Joad family to have campsites with flushing toilets, never before seen or used. It was the first time they were treated like decent human beings. When President Roosevelt took office, his first 100 days were spent in getting programs going, passing emergency laws, getting welfare programs started and Social Security was written into law in 1935. The WPA was established to put people to work and they hired my father. It was the beginning of many new programs and laws to make our country a better place.

In the 1960s, things changed. President Kennedy was assassinated and soon after that, his brother was also assassinated. Johnson was sworn into presidency. Our involvement, in what was considered an unnecessary long terrible war in Vietnam, brought a new era to our country including the hippie movement, long hair, as well as anti-war groups and drugs.

The movie, <u>Easy Rider</u> was such a movie. It was a period of time when the bike riders and drifters, on their way to nowhere and were involved with drugs. They were different, and in small towns, the local people do not take a liking to different people. One of the riders had long hair and they both dressed and acted differently from the locals. They were outcasts anywhere they rode. They were not even allowed to stay in motels because they were considered 'white-trash'.

<u>Grapes of Wrath</u> and <u>Bonnie and Clyde</u> were similar as far as the period of history is concerned. In <u>Grapes of Wrath</u>, many forms of violent treatment were used. They were treated like scum of the earth, which was not proper treatment for honest starving people. <u>Bonnie and Clyde</u> and parts of <u>Grapes of Wrath,</u> the brutality of <u>Easy Rider</u> ended when both bikers were shot and killed because they were considered outcasts.

September 3rd, 1998 Case-Work called:
PERSONAL CULTURAL ANALYSIS
[Editor's Note: The following appears in its original unedited form.]

My primary ethnic/racial heritage is German and Russian. My father was born on a small farm in New York State and my mother came to this country as a young girl of seven or eight. I do not know anything about my grandparents' heritage. We spoke English in our home and rarely, my parents spoke German to each other. The most important matter I can write about my heritage is not where my primary ethnic race originated from, but how poor we were. I was a little girl growing up in a family of four girls and two boys, my mother and father, and we were always hungry. There was not enough food to eat. My father was a sign painter and there were not many signs to paint. We did get assistance from the government so we could have some food. It was called 'government relief'.

When I was a young girl, there was no such thing as family communication. "Children were to be seen, but not heard." I recently completed a class on Family Communications that I found extremely valuable and could have used that knowledge while I was married. We need to communicate to each other in meaningful ways.

Our young lives growing up during the depression were ones of 'operation survival'. When a little girl and never having a doll in my life, I later became a doll collector and had about 400 dolls in what I called a beginner collection of whatever I could find at garage sales. I sold that collection for $1,000.00, which was insufficient. I now have a smaller collection in glass cabinets where they can be enjoyed.

The laws that became important to our lives and are still important are the Social Security Act of 1935. There are major problems with the old system and it must be changed before it goes broke. There were many other new laws for welfare assistance, old age and unemployment programs. During the administration of Franklin D. Roosevelt, it could all be summed up to what they called 'The New Deal'. Our country was in a state of disaster and many programs had to be put into effect to keep populations from starving and put the unemployed back to work.

The 'baby boomers' are coming of age and this out-dated system is not ready for the growing population of retirees. Other problems with the Social Security System are the life expectancy was not one of the growing older and older that is now happening. We are living longer because of new discoveries in health, welfare, education and technology. Other laws were the Civil Rights Act of 1964 outlawing racial and gender discrimination in employment. An Equal Employment Opportunities Commission was established. An important major law written was the Age Discrimination Employment Act of 1967. This one is very important to me as I am about to enter the job market again, and this time in a professional field of Human Services in some area of serving the elderly.

The dynamics and consequences of social and economic injustice, human oppression and discrimination experiences of my specific population were that I have learned the value of growing up in a time of hardships. I know how important it is to be able to work and make a living for your families. I know how important it is to become better educated. I know what it is to work and become independent and prosperous in our democratic society.

There are many opportunities in our country that should be appreciated and often are not. I am grateful for my decision to attend college in 1994. I am a first generation student and everyone in my primary family was proud of me. My sons were all supportive and they and my five grandchildren attended the graduation at NHCC in June of 1997 continuing at Metropolitan State University with a degree in Human Services with an emphasis on Gerontology.

Written for Family Communication on 4/13/1998

[Editor's Note: The following story appears in its original unedited form.]

Three Communication-Rules in my Family of Origin:

1. Children were to be seen, but not heard.
2. Our father was the boss. He made all the decisions.
3. Communication was not important between family members.

Our mother was the person that took care of all our needs, including most important, our father's needs. Communication was something we never did much of with our family. It was a terrible time in history, "The Great Depression of the 1930s" and there were many more important things than how we were going to communicate with each other as a family. Were we going to get enough to eat to keep us from being too hungry until the next meal? It was a time in history when some families were almost starving and eating was more important than talking. Of course, there was communication going on with my sisters. The communication was probably more of difficult times than ones of happy childhood days. When children are cold and hungry and do not know why and the parents are not communicating with their children, a certain part of your whole life is one of unhappy memories.

My father did not talk with us very often and I

cannot remember any real conversations with him when I was a child. I cannot remember any loving relationships with my family until many years later and our family relationships remained distant. These rules changed when I was married. I found communication to be of major importance. It is the only way two persons can get to know each other. However, it was in the period of time when men were in charge. They did not say so in verbal ways, but it was understood. In the military, it would be considered that husbands were the commanders and the wives, first officers.

When our sons were growing up Cliff and I was always busy working, I was the one in charge of our family communications. If anything major needed to be solved, then Cliff was the person that handled the problem. We discussed the solutions between Cliff and me, but Cliff's decision was the one we followed. I let this controlling continue. It was the 'father knew best' era. Our sons did not have choices. The rules were made for them. The best thing that ever happened is that rules are made to be broken. As our sons grew older, they no longer wanted to be placed into a rigid space without family communication.

Cliff and I were always busy working with our businesses, there was little time left for good family communication skills and we all lacked so much in the communication department. It was like the book, Ordinary People. Family communication is necessary. We said many unimportant words without solid family communicating. (What a waste?)

Both Cliff and I grew up in the same period of time and families did not discuss many things with their siblings. It was the time that men were considered more important than women. They were only good for certain things such as wives, mothers, and persons for nurturing families. Women were not supposed to be thinking, discussing, and changing ideas that were not their concerns.

Yes, our communication patterns have changed. Since my divorce in 1991, communications with my sons has been more meaningful. I am so thankful our times have changed in every way. Children are now a major part of the system, as well as all extended family members. Everyone must be involved and encouraged to participate in the functioning of the always changing-family mobile system.

Dying – (My friend Lucy)
Journal Writing Class 8/27/1998
[Editor's Note: The following story appears in its original unedited form.]

Each day I visited Lucy at the <u>Maranatha Nursing Home</u> in Brooklyn Center, Minnesota. I saw her change from a very sick person to one that was dying. We had been close friends for four years.

She was a pretty woman, full of life and loved to dance. Each week, she had her hair done in the salon at JCPenney's in the Brookdale Mall, and would always stop and see me while I was at work. We would go dancing at least once each week or more. She met her friend Les at the VFW while we were together. He was a good dancer and continued seeing him. Lucy had two beautiful large Persian Cats she loved, owned a beautiful large town-home in Brooklyn Center and had been divorced for years. We loved dancing at the VFW 109, in New Brighton because they had a good band and over 100 persons attending, including many singles.

I took Lucy 200 miles north to visit her Aunt and her two godchildren. We spent the day where she grew up as a child. This was the longest drive I had ever made, in one long day and both enjoyed the day enormously.

Lucy had cancer several different times and each time the doctors thought they got it all, but never did. I remember all the chemo and radiation treatments she endured. She was determined to survive her cancer. In 1998, doctors could no longer cure Lucy and it continued to spread rapidly throughout her body. One day coming from a job interview dressed in the best business suit owned, stopped to see her. She was in a special dining room where patients had to be fed and I did. She looked at me with a dying, sad expression. It made me feel extremely uncomfortable. It was like she was thinking, why was she dying and why could it not be me instead. Anyway I finished feeding her and told her I would see her again soon. It had been extremely stressful to watch all her hair fall out, she could no longer talk and her body had become weaker and she seemed to be approaching death.

The next few days, I went back to the nursing home to visit Lucy. I went directly to her room after signing the registry of guests. When I arrived, the bed was empty and it had been made up. I went to the nurses' station to ask where my friend Lucy was. They told me she died during the night. It was a strange feeling, but I left the nursing home somewhat angry. Les should have called me to let me know she died. I was one of the few persons that visited her often.

This death touched me deeply while attending college, trying to do homework and visiting my dying friend. Soon after, I attended her funeral with Les. She was cremated. I said the eulogy at her funeral including, about how much she enjoyed life and the times we spent together. To this day, I will always remember my friend, Lucy and to be emotionally involved in the dying process of someone close is never forgotten.

Graduation from North Hennepin
Community College in 1997

Back to School – Conclusion

No amount of words can describe my feelings
for having the opportunity to attend college and
completing this journey into the field of a 'higher
education'. I am delighted to have succeeded as
an unconventional student. I was eager to learn so
many things that I did not know and I continue to
be thankful for the time that was devoted to this
challenge. I cannot help feeling joy in taking on
this struggle, journeying towards success in earning both my AA and BA Degrees. Yes, I am proud
of myself, every single day.

I wish to conclude with "A gigantic thank you,
to all my professors for the part they played in
assisting me. This accomplishment, without a
doubt was one of enormous rewards of my lifetime." Another page of my life has been turned.

The Big Move

So much was happening so fast. I was taken to the Unity Hospital after calling 911 that afternoon because my blood pressure had gone up to an extremely high level of 211 over 116 and I had a terrible pressure in my head. After being in the emergency room for two and a half hours, I was released. It became scary living alone.

My son Richard and his wife Bonnett encouraged me to consider moving close to them or close to Greg and Sherry. After spending a day with Richard and Bonne and looking at what the town had to offer and considering the possibilities of living close to them, I decided that I would prefer to live closer to Greg and Sherry for a number of reasons, including more mild winter weather and to be closer to my two grandchildren, Dakota and Matthew.

Several months later, I took a trip to Illinois and looked at condominiums in Kingston and in the city of Rockford. After a lot of indecision between two different homes, I made and offer on a house. At first, the owners didn't want to accept my offer, but eventually things were worked out and I bought the home I now own.

I had to sell my town-home quickly and Lotte Seidler of Coldwell Banker became the realtor and it took only two days to sell. The value of my home had gone up unbelievably and I received a large check for my equity and made other arrangements to cash out of some mutual funds and paid for my home in full. Even though my house is completely paid for, I no longer feel financially secure, and now have to be concerned with every dollar spent for the rest of my life.

There were so many things to do before I moved, like giving notice at my part-time job working for a plumbing contractor employer, which was difficult. They did not want me to move because I was writing the first newsletter they ever had and we were on our fourth issue. The plumbing company, including the office staff and plumbers enjoyed this newsletter and I loved writing it. I was assigned other interesting work besides and paid $11.00 per hour. I never earned as much as that again.

Packing boxes took over my life and I eliminated years of accumulated junk. Each day was spent packing and getting ready for this move. Greg came to help, but only had two days available because he was scheduled for school in Denver to become licensed to fly the Airbus as a Captain. It was terrific to have his help and he accomplished more for me than I would have in a few weeks of working alone. We stacked and labeled items in all of the rooms. He took back a truckload of stuff that the movers would not take, including plants, computer, and cement blocks.

Richard and Bonne generously drove their car and mine to Illinois in order to save me a large fee that the moving company was going to charge to tow my car to Illinois. My grandson Grant also went along and visited his cousins overnight before they drove back to Minnesota the next day.

On July 17th, 2001, I wrote, "This is the last full day in my home that has been mine for nearly six years. Everything is packed except for some vitamins, a spoon, fork, knife and teapot and in the bedroom, the bedding, telephone, clock, radio, mouthwash and toothbrush. It looks like I'm ready to go. I'm dressed in my best beige shorts and tee shirt and vest. My best friend, Diana is taking me to dinner at 5:30pm and to see her new apartment. After more than ten years of friendship, we will say goodbye."

The next morning, I wrote, "It's 9:10am, Wednesday and I'm sitting here on my blue recliner while I still have one, watching the four person crew take my home apart. They are carried my curio out and I was afraid to watch. All the dining room chairs are gone. I found a few dead, dried up bugs lying around. I carefully picked them up to put them in the trash. The trash bag is in the sink so it will not be hauled to Morning Glory Lane in Loves Park, IL. There goes the beautiful hope chest I bought a few years ago, which is a collectable and has a unique picture painted on the front showing what JCPenney looked like in 1902. They just took my blue recliner and my TV away. I now know what a displaced person is, without a home. What a job this has been!

The last three weeks of life was spent packing. "Yes, I'm really moving and leaving Minnesota forever. My car had been left at our friend's, the Sterner's in Brooklyn Center, for Richard and Bonne to pickup in a few days. Betty drove me to the hotel for the night and we had dinner together. The Coldwell Banker Realtor, Lotte Seidler picked me up for the closing in the morning then drove me to the airport to fly to Chicago. After arriving in Chicago, I took a shuttle bus to the City of Rockford.

On July 19th, I wrote, "I do not live in Minnesota anymore. I am now a resident of Loves Park, IL after the closing on the new town-home. The realtor from Whitehead Realtors, Doris Ullrich, picked me up at the bus depot. She arranged for my hotel room, took me to dinner, picked me up and took me to the bank to open an account and many other wonderfully helpful things to make my a little easier. Packing and unpacking boxes seemed to take forever. I never want to move again for the rest of my life. Another page in my life has been turned.

My Basement History Wall

I decided to enjoy my basement. It is a terrific room with a cheerful and warm feeling to it. I know why my grandchildren enjoy this room so much.

In the 1970's, I created stuff of interest to me. One day, I acted on an idea I had and mod-podged, <u>TIME</u> Magazine covers onto plywood panels. I did that on two panels, which were installed in the basement wall next to a huge bookcase, on the farm in Cushing, MN. I feel that it looked great and I was very proud of that wall.

After much time elapsed, I requested that these panels be given to me, as I knew that Cliff and his new wife Leone were remodeling their home and they were not likely to keep them. Jim graciously used his small truck to bring them to my townhouse in Brooklyn Park, where they were stored for a while in my garage. They were laying sideways with the finished side showing. Every morning when I was on my way to work, I would look at those old mod-podged panels that had been done in the 70's, and would say to myself, "Millie, that's your life laying against that garage wall". What a gruesome thought that was!

When I was moving from Brooklyn Park to my new home in Loves Park, IL, When Greg was helping me and had his truck bed fully loaded. At the last minute, he asked if I was going to take those mod-podged panels and I said, "Yes." He loaded them last to cover everything in the truck bed and then strapped everything down. My two panels then went to Greg and Sherry's garage in Kingston, Illinois.

After thirty years and much moving, they were dirty and looked terrible. One day, I decided I wanted Greg to bring my two plywood Time cover panels to my new home in Loves Park, which he did. We cleaned off each panel before carrying them to my basement. Greg had placed them upright on the wall where they would eventually be permanently placed and I was immediately motivated to do more with them. Greg said, "They look a whole lot better on your basement wall than they did in my garage." Now they were clean, but still in need of repairing. I slowly made the repairs over the next two years.

I was so excited about those walls, I decided I would do some more of them. Greg bought me three panels of plywood and had to cut them because they were too long for my basement wall. He also brought his two metal sawhorses to use, so I could work on the new wall in the basement and on April 12th, 2003, I wrote the ending to this story.

After two more years, I have completed two walls of 'NEWSWEEK' covers. Greg has placed them upright on one of my walls. The other two walls from the 1970's are quite a contrast from the two new ones of the 2000's. I call these walls 'My History Walls.'

During the month of November, the Machesney Park Mall had a huge Antique sale. I happened to see some large 1968 Normal Rockwell prints of President Reagan, Nixon, and Johnson and some others of Hubert Humphrey, Bobby Kennedy and Eugene McCarthy and a print of Martin Luther King, Jr., photographed by Carl Bernstein for 'Look' Magazine, done sometime in the 1960's. I bought them all and with Greg's help, they were placed on an opposite wall and shortly after, another section of Newsweek covers were added. The last one included Saddam Husseim coming out of his 'spider hole' saying, "Don't Shoot, I'm the President of Iraq." That he will never be again. "We Got Him."

9.11, A New Kind of War

Returning from a 25-minute walk on a beautiful bright day in our community of 'Preservation Pointe Condominiums' in Loves Park, it was a time for exercising and thinking. "How lucky we are to be living in a free society among a world of many places that were not free or decent places to live."

Yesterday, September 11th, 2001, all 'Hell broke loose' in the largest city in our country, and in the world. It was like an Armageddon – Was it a modern day 'Pearl Harbor?"

The day started out as a normal day for four large commercial flights - two from 'American Airlines' and two from 'United Airlines. The pilots were doing their regular jobs, flying passengers to their destinations. These four planes were 'High-jacked' and taken over by mid-eastern terrorists. Their plan was to seize the largest aircraft, the ones carrying enormous loads of jet fuel. This terrorist attack was skillfully planned and carried out.

Two planes were rerouted to fly directly into the tallest buildings into the 'World Trade Center Twin Towers' of New York City, while these building were filled with thousands of working people. Thousands of people were killed including everyone on all four or the planes. It was a major disaster in our lives that will never go away.

Many of the persons in the buildings, including firemen and other rescue workers, doing their jobs trying to save people, were among the many to die or become seriously injured. The buildings crumpled quickly while many people were running for their lives, down thousands of stairs while trying to get out in time. Some people were jumping out of the windows with no chance for survival. The Mayor of New York City, Rudy Giuliani, went into action trying to calm the city with his unforgettable leadership throughout the worst terrorist disaster ever to be committed.

Today's technology allowed the whole world to watch these sudden explosions and it was a brutal vision for every viewer. Was this real and why should it happen? The media alerted us another plane was heading for Washington, DC and flew into the Pentagon, killing more people and we were told that another plane might be heading towards the White House.

The President was in Florida attending a school event with young children when he received the news. The Secret Service quickly escorted our President away and he was flown to Los Angeles. Air Force One became 'the flying White House'. Then they flew on to Omaha, Nebraska to a bunker, keeping in touch with his administration until it was considered safe for him to return to the White House. Many Staff members at the Capitol were evacuated into the depths of the White House where our Vice-President, Dick Cheney and the Secretary of Defense, Donald Rumsfeld, made decisions based on this national emergency.

We had some heroic people on board the fourth plane, which was likely to be crashed into the White House. Several heroic persons lead the challenge. After saying some goodbyes on their cell phones, one of them said "Let's roll." They then apparently fought with the high-jackers and in doing so the plane crashed in a field in Pennsylvania, saving our nation's, White House. These brave Americans are real heroes who we can all be grateful for.

All air traffic was requested to immediately land at the nearest airport. My son, Greg was flying a United Airplane that morning. His wife Sherry had just talked with him a short time before takeoff, but did not ask him where his destination was. She had no idea where he might be heading when the Trade Towers were hit. I was with Sherry that morning because we were going shopping. She was very scared for everyone, especially Greg. Their children also knew their dad was flying.

Greg was grounded in Indianapolis for four days. He was ordered to stay with his Airbus. It became stressful because they were not giving the pilots any news about what was going on or any idea when they would be able to return with their planes.

The Wall Street Markets closed. It was a time for mourning over loss of life and for victim's families. The entire free world shared in our grief. After a few days of chaos, we were told to go on with our lives and 'business as usual'. In our minds, it would never again be business as usual.

The terrorist plans were skillfully created and unbelievable. It took our top officials only a very short time to be sure it was Osama bin Laden who was responsible. The problem is we do not know where he is hiding and someday, we will find him, "Dead or Alive", and bring him to justice.

It was a time for mourning this horrible tragedy. Never in our lives have we ever experienced any one attacking us in our own country. It was not only the loss of innocent lives for our country, but a loss for other countries, as their citizens were also working in the World Trade Center Towers, making this a disaster for the entire world.

The costs were enormous and we had no idea what the amount could be. How do you put a dollar value on human lives? The airlines suffered major losses that helped put United Airlines into bankruptcy, causing their employees to lose all of their retirement stocks and take many cuts in pay in order to survive.

"We are all going through this together," one young man said as he left his church service on September 16th 2001. We can no longer take freedom for granted. President, George W. Bush and staff, the New York Mayor, journalists, firemen and law enforcing persons were doing tremendous amounts of work to do whatever had to be done. Persons looking for loved ones seemed to continue doing that for a long time. Every one was brought together helping each other to cope with disaster and loss of life.

After living through the Great Depression, World War II, Vietnam, the Persian Gulf War and now this new type of Terrorist war, like no war that has ever been fought before, it was frightening. I will watch, learn, hope and pray that our world will again, some day be free from terrorists and that night I went to bed afraid.

On September 20, 2001, the President addressed the nation. It was important for us American people hear words to make some sense of this tragedy from the leader of our nation... words to make us understand about this new and very real threat from terrorists. We had little knowledge of this kind of war, because we had never experienced it in our country before. He had to deliver a message that would make us feel confident in our future.

We knew it would be a long and complicated war. His speech to Congress and everyone in the world was powerful. He ended with, "I have a message for our military – Be Ready." The military reserve had been called to serve. We hoped to have the support of other free countries, both financially and militarily. This was a new kind of war, with terrorists willing to die to accomplish their missions. It is hard to know how, when and where the next target may be. Our free democratic society has been raided and will never be the same again.

It has made our skies less safe and created major costly changes. It used to be called 'The Friendly Skies' and now it is no longer that. I am sometimes afraid for my son, Greg's safety. Terrorism is a very complicated situation that has to be solved. It could happen again at any time and at any place in our country or any other free country in the world.

Air Traffic Controllers
Helping The Skies Be Safer

One event that aired on an NBC Special with Tom Brokaw, a year after 9.11 was about how the morning of 9.11 unfolded for air traffic controller.

"Traffic controllers were in tears, shaking and crying. They were losing the airplanes in the sky and had no communication with these planes. They knew something was terribly wrong. Managers of the controllers were immediately brought in to help. Washington, DC was contacted. It was awful.

There were thousands of planes that had to be cleared out of the skies, immediately. Around the time of the Pentagon crash, all airplanes were directed to land at the closest airports. The controllers did not know if anymore buildings would be blown up at that time."

"The show showed the viewers what the sky looked like with dots marking the airplanes in flight. The controllers had to clear planes from the sky at about one every second. What a time the controllers had all over the country to get all the planes down as fast as they could. One of the controllers told Tom Brokaw, "I fell apart after completing this job. I was shaking and crying uncontrollable tears."

This was the story we hadn't been told to my knowledge. Thanks to Tom Brokaw for this terrific and amazing NBC Special, which was astonishing to hear and view. This story showed the audience the major part our air traffic controllers play in running our skies safely. It was an important news story for everyone and especially one of personal interest to me. My son, Greg, as Captain is responsible for every passenger flying in his plane for United Airlines.

News Story Writing

I continued writing. First I wrote two newsletters for our 109 Condominium complex at Preservation Pointe Association, where I resided. They authorized two issues, because of their limited funds. I decided to rewrite my favorite story in the last newsletter for the Post Journal, a weekly publication for the Loves Park and Machesney Park area. His story was important because of my personal family involvement with flying.

Loves Park couple really enjoys the wild blue yonder Carroll Dietz with his Hatz bi-plane.
(Photo taken by Mike Ruggles)

Loves Park couple really enjoys the wild blue yonder

By: Millie Chandler for the Post Journal–
Published 8/8/2002

[Editor's Note: The following story appears in its original published version]

Carroll Dietz's love for flying has always been a major part of his life. He can be seen approximately two to three times a week taking off in his open cockpit, BI-Plane from the Poplar Grove Airport located approximately ten miles from his home at Preservation Pointe Condominiums in Loves Park.

"I started flying when I was 18 years old and as soon as I left home, so my Mother would not know I was flying," said Dietz.

In 1947, he joined the U. S. Airforce, and stayed in four years. Then he returned to being a civilian again and in 1951, Carroll met his mate, the other Carol.

When asked where they met, Carol said, "We met in an Alley." After some laughter following that statement, she went on to say, "Incidentally, it happened to be a Bowling Alley." On June 7, 1952, they were married, making their first home in Lombard, IL. Dietz was employed at Mitchel Field as an Aircraft Mechanic.

In 1955, Dietz was hired by Eastern Airlines. Throughout the years, he later became Captain flying a DC 10 to South America and London until retiring in 1988.

In 1963, at age thirty-four, Dietz's greatest desire was to own an airplane. However, none he looked at suited him and he decided to build his own plane. He said, "I decided my plane would be red and white, and I purchased a plan and all the materials I would need. The car came out of the garage and in came all the needed materials. It was a small one-seat plane so it fit." Approximately three years later, my beautiful BI-Plane, after the proper aircraft inspection, was ready to fly. I may have been the happiest person alive."

The experience of building his own plane continued to delight him. He decided to build another just like the other one, and then he continued to fly both planes for the next eight years.

The love of flying continues to run in his family. One son Jeff has been flying with Northwest Airlines since 1979 and is a Captain, flying a 747. Another son, Dale, has been with United Airlines since 1989 and is flying a 737 out of O'Hare Airport. A third son, Steve, is a private pilot and flies a Luscome.

"A few months ago, my youngest son, Steve spotted a BI-Plane in Warroad, MN", said Dietz. "This 1980 plane was called Hatz, and it was for sale. He immediately thought his Dad would not be able to live without this plane. Arrangements to see this BI-Plane were made, and I became the new owner." This plane is Dietz's newest joy in his life, and he keeps it hangered at the Poplar Grove Airport located in Poplar Grove, IL.

Planes aren't the only way the Dietzs travel. They have had four motor homes since the 1990's. They traveled around the country in a 38-foot Newmar Dutch Star motor home.

"It had everything in it including a Queen size bed in the bedroom, two television sets and everything you need to make living easy," said Carol. "Living in a motor home beats staying in Motels. Traveling in them is better than flying because you have too many delays of waiting. We have visited many places including Alaska and a number of National Parks, and it is the experience of a life time meeting wonderful people all the time."

In November of 2001, they purchased their new home at Preservation Pointe Condominiums in Loves Park, IL, and later sold their diesel motor home.

On June 7, 2002, it was the Dietz's 50th Wedding Anniversary. "Our family of four sons and two daughters and 13 grandchildren are scattered all over the East Coast to the West Coast and nothing was planned," said Carol. "We decided to go to dinner at Timberman's in East Dubque, IL. A few days later, we 'hit the road' with our packed suitcases and headed south to Memphis. We had a great time." Carol pointed to the framed layout on the living room wall and said, "Our daughter-in-law, Sandy, had created this specially framed setting with the gold engraved 50th wedding anniversary on it by using our recent studio portrait and a couple of our old wedding photos. We are both very proud of our treasured gift."

On July 24, 2002, Carroll Dietz joined his son, Steve, in Oshkosh, WI for their annual EAA (Experimental Aircraft Association) Fly-In. It is an event that he has been attending since 1963. "Flying has been the main part of my life for over 50 years," said Dietz, "combined with the 50 wonderful years of marriage and family."

Another favorite story published by the Journal was about mall walking because my love for mall walking, which I have been doing more than 12 years. I have met many friends while mall walking.

MALL WALKERS - (front row–left to right)
Nancy Knauss, Shirley Ling, and Darlene Washington,
(back row)
(Nell Isom, Jerry Green, Kathlean Kaltved,
Debbie Stasica, and Avis Stasica

Walking at Machesney Park Mall proves popular exercise

By: Millie Chandler for the Journal
Published on September 5, 2002.
[Editor's Note: The following story appears in its original, published version]

Every day walkers can be seen at Machesney Park Mall, a terrific place for walking, as well as shopping. If a person walks from JCPenney Outlet Store to Bergner's, including every corridor, the distance is .8 of one mile. A walker doing this five times would've completed a four-mile walk. Most of the faster mall walkers do that in approximately one hour.

According to <u>The President's Council on Physical Fitness and Sports</u>, 165 million American adults, age's range from18 and older are walking for exercise and that number is increasing every year. Mall walking is the most popular form of exercise.

In a national survey, the highest percentage of regular walkers was found to be among persons 65 years of age and older. Walking continues in it's popularity because of health-giving qualities and walking for pleasure where many new friendships are made.

<u>Jerry Green</u> resides in Machesney Park and began walking approximately five months ago. "I started walking because I have osteoporosis and my Doctor told me that walking is a bone jarring exercise that will strengthen your bones. That was a good enough reason for me to mall walk. Since I started to walk, I have lost 31 lbs. I never had the opportunity to walk before because I was always working in a difficult job." She added, "I walk from five to seven days a week. After my walk, I feel much better. I'm refreshed and ready to start my day," said Green.

<u>Shirley Ling</u> residing in the Forest View Community in Machesney Park with her husband of many years was another walker that was talked

with. "I have been mall walking for approximately 10 years. I have an artificial prosthesis above my knee," said Ling.

"In 1950, at age 18, I was married and soon after, in 1951, a cancerous growth was discovered in the back of the right knee and at age 19, my left leg had to be removed from above the knee." She was soon fitted with an artificial prosthesis and had to learn to walk again.

Ling has two grown children and two grand children. Sometime in 1994, she started walking in the mall. She walks approximately 1 fi miles each day. She went on to say, "Sometimes getting going in the morning is difficult, but I feel so much better after I have completed my walk. I enjoy the people and getting to know other people, including the walkers and the store people.

I feel this mall is a very friendly place to shop and walk. I have had no further occurrence of the cancer and each day, I give credit to God."

Darlene Washington, an Avon representative for 23 years, residing in Loves Park said, "I like walking at Machesney Park Mall because the temperature is always great for walking and there are no dogs to bite you while you walk. I have made many friends at the mall. I have been a mall walker for at least 10 years. Walking is something I do for me and it makes me feel good."

Kathleen Kaltved, residing in Machesney Park was our next walker. She said, "I have been walking in this mall for approximately five years and walk every weekday, sometimes from four to six times around." She is an excellent fast walker. Kaltved went on to say, "I have four grown children, 12 grandchildren and five great grandchildren, all babies.

I was a War Bride and met my husband Willis while he was in the Army in Ardlfe, South Wales, which is part of the United Kingdom, near London. We married in England in 1946 until Willis passed away 11 years ago." She continued, "Walking has become an important part of my life and I have met many people in the mall, including the ones in the Machesney Mall stores. I have had several problems with my back and a 'pinched nerve' in my left leg, including osteoporosis. Walking is beneficial for everything in our lives."

Our final walkers talked with were a mother, Avis Istasica, and her daughter, Debbie, age 45, both reside in Loves Park. They walk separately because Debbie walks at a faster pace than her mother. They have been walking this mall for over two years. Avis said, "I walk to keep active and to maintain good health and I have more energy." She is the mother of five grown children, six grandchildren, and three great grandchildren. Debbie said, "I walk five to six times around. It motivates me to see others, both younger persons and older persons walking. I do it because it is helping to keep my blood pressure down. After my daily walk, I feel a sense of accomplishment."

The following was a special story and I was pleased to have the opportunity to write it and have it published. Tom and Mary Guyer were extremely happy with their story and they purchased 30 newspapers from the Journal.

Survival, sharing, devotion and love in Loves Park

By Millie Chandler for the Journal
Published on Dec, 5, 2002
[Editor's Note: The following story appears in its original, published version]

"Partially due to our aging population, kidney disease has become the ninth leading cause of death and one of the most expensive chronic diseases to treat. Approximately 75 million Americans are at risk due to a number of factors, including diabetes, high blood pressure, inherited and congenital kidney diseases and other factors." (Quoted from 'Facts about Kidney Disease')

"According to the National Institutes of Health, about 100,000 Americans are diagnosed with total and permanent kidney failure or end-stage renal disease (ESRD) and must go on dialysis or undergo a transplant of a healthy kidney in order to live." This is the reason that Mary and Tom Guyer of Loves Park are sharing their story.

In 1971 they both worked at John S. Barnes, making pumps for various types of machinery and Mary's job was on assembly work. That year Tom enlisted in the Air Force and was discharged in 1973. He returned to his former company continuing in the engineering department.

Through an introduction of friends while employed there, Tom and Mary started to date, and became engaged on May Day. The wedding took place on September 1, 1973 in Rockford and they moved to Loves Park in 1977. They have been married for twenty-nine years.

In 1975, Mary attended Beauty School and became a Hair Stylist and was employed in several shops in Rockford. Then later, she returned to Beauty School again and obtained a Cosmetology Instructors License. Then continued her career in other schools teaching students to become stylists. She later opened her own shop business in the neighborhood.

Tom is employed for Textron in Rockford and works in the Shipping Department. Tom's hobbies are bow hunting, fishing, and woodworking, maintaining all repairs, and remodeling for their home. They both love camping in their RV Popup that fits their needs perfectly and their favorite camping ground is Yukon Camping Resort in Lyndon Station, WI.

During the early 1990's, Mary started to have some serious health problems and in 1998, at age

47, she needed a hip replacement. She was told it resulted from prescribed medications, which were causing her body to experience difficulty in walking. After the hip replacement, it took her nearly one year to be able to walk again. At times, walking continues to be challenging and at times painful.

After several years, her specialist revealed another serious health problem and was told she would need a kidney transplant and a donor. In 1999, Mary and Tom were both tested to see if he was a match. A week later they received the results and learned that he could be her donor.

Tom & Mary Guyer
Photo by Millie Chandler

At that time, Mary was not experiencing sufficient reactions from her kidneys to warrant a transplant. Mary's mother was not considered a donor because she was age 81, one brother only had one kidney, and her other brother was not considered for health reasons.

A few years later, it was necessary for this surgery. The kidney transplant took place on July 10,

2002 at UW Health Hospitals and Clinic in Madison, Wisconsin. Mary's husband was the donor. The surgery took four hours to remove Tom's left kidney for Mary's transplant. After four days of recovery, Tom was released from the hospital feeling good. Mary's surgery followed Tom's, and her procedure also took four hours. The first few days after surgery were taking longer for her to recover. "While I was coming out of recovery, and could focus, the first person I remember seeing was Tom checking up on me and my heart seemed to fill me with devotion and love for him," said Mary.

"It was the most wonderful thing I have ever been able to do in my life to give a kidney to my beloved wife and our second chance for our continued years together," said Tom. A week later, Mary was released from the hospital. Everyday continues to be a stepping stone to recovery. "Become a donor, because it may be the best and only chance you have in your life to keep another person alive," said Tom. "Not a day goes by that we both think about this bond of sharing the gift of life," said Mary.

… … … …

I valued writing this story of Michael's success. It was difficult to organize all the information and write. It left me feeling good to be the journalist writing and sharing his personal story of accomplishment.

Michel Humpal

Michael Humpal rides to success by overcoming health problems
By Millie Chandler for the Journal
published 1/23/2003
[Editor's note: The following story appears in its original, published version]

It's hard to become a top athlete. It's even harder when you have to overcome illness to do so. However, that's what Machesney Park's Michel L. Humpal has been able to accomplish.

In September 2002 Humpal entered "the Largest Bike Race in the World," in Cable, Wisconsin. This race was called the "Chequmegon Fat Tire Festival: Humpal finished only 30 seconds behind a racer that the U. S. Olympic Committee sent to Australia to represent the United States in the World Championship.

That was quite a change from the way things were for Humpal for much of his life.

The Humpal family resided in the Rockford area all their lives and for the last 10 years has lived in Machesney Park. From his infancy, Michael L. Humpal developed a severe case of Asthma and many allergies and needed constant treatment and was prescribed excessive amounts of medication through age 16 for both conditions. The doctors cautiously advised what activities he could and could not participate in while enrolled in school.

"I could not go out and play with the other school children and it made me feel like I was not quite normal. At times I did not get to participate and when I did, I found myself not keeping up with the other kids my age. I was usually 'huffing and puffing' and ended up with trips to the Nurse's Office," said Humpal.

In 1989, at age 7, Mike started racing in the BMX (bicycle) Races but always came in dead last. He did not like being a looser, so he gave up racing bikes.

He started working with his Dad in the bicycle business when he was in the sixth grade. Young Mike especially liked it because instead of doing chores at home, he worked in his Dad's store putting bicycles together and was paid small amounts of money for his work. He helped out in all his spare time and on weekends

Beginning Junior High, the Humpal's moved to Machesney Park and Mike was enrolled at Harlem Junior High. He continued to be heavily medicated for his severe Asthma and allergies. There were lasting effects to his entire body. Humpal wanted to be a player in many sports and participated in baseball, basketball, and skateboarding.

"By the time I was a teenager, I knew the signs of my coming Asthma attacks. I would stop and slow down before they were out of control. My friends accepted my physical condition and they were often supportive. However, team playing was another thing. The other kids gave me dirty looks, like I should not be there and finally I no longer wanted to deal with being an unwanted team player," said Humpal.

While a student, Humpal had some interest in artwork but liked sports much more then school. He and a few friends loved skateboarding causing him to break his left arm, not once, but twice and had to have re-constructive surgery. "Now I have four metal plates holding that arm together," said Humbal. That was the end of Humpal's skateboarding career.

When between the ages of 15 and 16, Humpal had many health problems getting sick again with his Asthma. He returned to his Doctor to see what could be done to improve his health condition. He was informed the medication he was taking was not appropriate for his sporting activities, effecting his reflexes, and that was what caused him to break his arm.

"Being the 'rebel teenager' I was, I said, the heck with it. I'm done with taking all this medication," said Humpal. That was the last time he ever took any medicine for his allergies and Asthma. Humpal was 17. His decision changed his life.

In 1997, he started to pick up on Mountain Bike Group riding at Rock Cut State Park. The group riding lasted until 1999 and then it was dissolved because most of the group were adult riders and seemed to have more important things to do. Two years of Mountain Bike Riding left Humpal in love with riding.

In 2000 at Rock Cut Park, Humpal entered his first cross-country riding race. He finished sixth out of approximately 30 riders in the 10-mile event. "It was a big deal because my father was there and the excitement I saw from him made me feel like I finally found something I was good at," said Humpal.

When Mike first started riding there were no major plans for racing but he continued to ride during the week and started to race on weekends. That year he finished second place as a 'Novice Rider' in the Wisconsin 'Off Road Series'.

In 2001, Humpal graduated from Harlem High. That was when he started to hear about the other races in various parts of the country and then moved up another category in the racing series – 'Sport Level'. In that category, he did not do as well and was considered only average. It was a huge learning year for Humpal.

However, Humpal decided to set an unrealistic goal for himself. "I wanted to finish in first place in all the 'Expert Races' even though I did not belong there. I started to ride and ride and ride, approximately 30 hours per week. I figured that was the only way I would get better to keep riding and get faster," said Humpal.

"By that point in time, I knew my competition and made a list of roughly 20 of the fastest riders out of the 150 riders that would be a problem. I checked all the information on those top riders and compared their statistics to mine to figure out what I needed to work on to beat them. I had to treat racing like a chess game that would give me an edge to winning," he continued.

During the 2002 season, he moved up to the 'Expert Group' like he wanted to. The first six races of the season came easy and Mike won every one. After that, he fell into a slump period.

"I was approached by Jeff Otto, who offered to coach and teach me what I was missing and train me correctly, Otto turned me around and I started to win again," said Humpal.

It was time for 'Nationals' and Humpal finished in second place for the 'Wisconsin Nationals' and continued to race in both the 'Illinois and

Wisconsin Series'.

"I drove out to Durango, Colorado with a few other racers, but had a bad day and ended up in the eighth place. Because of the previous 'Nationals' I completed and the 'Wisconsin Series', they placed me in 'First Place' in the 'National Racing'. I completed the 'Illinois Series' with two wins, The 'Illinois State Championship' and the 'Illinois Series Champion Titles'," said Humpal.

He has participated in approximately 90 races all over the country and has received many trophies. His 'Sponsor' is Litespeed Bicycles from the State of Tennessee.

Humpal still works with his Dad and they take turns with managing <u>Humpal's Bicycle & Hobby Center</u> at Machesney Park Mall.

··· ··· ··· ···

The following story made page one. It was prior to the time our country was preparing for war against Saddam Husseim's regime. Our country's economy was a mess, we were on 'high alert' for terrorism, and war seemed very likely.

Seniors tell their concerns

By Millie Chandler for the Journal – 2/27/2003

[Editor's note: The following story appears in its original, published version]

When asked the question, "What are your most important concerns or issues today?" Here are the answers from the persons talked with.

Dale Morrison, a retired construction worker, resides on the west side of the Rockford area with his wife, Mary and I have been married for forty years. He is a mall walker and comes to Machesney Park Mall six days a week.

"My most important concern is for my daughter, Sgt. Robin Weaver, U.S. Army Reserves. She has been in the reserves for the past 18 years and was stationed at Freeport Base in the Military Police Unit. They are being sent to Fort McCoy, WI for further training and from there will be transferred to wherever they are needed. Robin is the mother of our two grandchildren. Billy, 15, in 10th Grade, and Melanie, 11 and in the 5th Grade and are both A students. Our son-in-law, Bill, Maintenance Technician for Motorola will be the remaining parent taking care of the family while Robin serves with the U. S. Army Reserves," said Morrison. "In 1994, one of our sons while serving in the U. S. Navy stationed in New Jersey, was ran over by a drunk driver and Dale, Jr., was killed at age 24," he continued. Their daughter, Jeannie, served with the Regular Navy for 12 years and oldest son, Tyler is retired from the U. S. Regular Navy after 20 years of service. Another son, Lonnie was in the Navy for four years. The Morrison family knows the true meaning of 'Serving our country'.

Audrey Jacobson & Margaret Johnson are sisters, both from the Rockford area, but drive to Machesney Park Mall a few times each week because it is the most convenient mall for them to walk, visit and shop. "Paying for medicine and looking forward to some new laws from Congress for assistance with the growing costs of prescription drugs is my most important concern," said Jacobson.

"I want to remain fully independent while continually, being able to pay all my bills and maintaining my home and yard for a long time. I value my independence," said Margaret Johnson.

Bob & Jerry Green of Machesney Park, were contacted next. "We have two grandsons serving in the U. S. Air Force. Our most important concern is our country's plans for this terrible war with Iraq. A very large number of our Armed Forces will be participating in this war. It will be extremely dangerous and we are upset and afraid some of our young men and women in service may never return," said Jerry Green.

Harold Richmond and his wife, Shirley resides in Loves Park and have been married for 51 years. Their family consists of five children, 10 grandchildren and three great grandchildren, all residing in this area. Richmond is a retired trucker. "Health issues are my most important concern and the rising high costs of medicines, both my wife and I need to maintain our health. I am looking forward to Legislation being passed concerning assistance with needed prescription costs for seniors," said Richmond.

B.J. (Barbara) Knickerbocker of Loves Park was talked with and her comments were as follows. "The high alert status our country is now in disturbs me. I have a very deep concern that our country will be going to war soon. All the troubling problems our country and the world are now facing with terrorists and this war, we do not know where or when some tragic event could happen and that is extremely frightening. I'm concerned for my grandchildren growing up in this dreadful uncertain world," said Knickerbocker.

Russell Lewis from Loves Park comes to Machesney Park Mall to walk and meet with his friends. He is a retired trucker with Teamsters Local. He has six grown children; seven grandchildren and most of his family live in this area.

"I am trying to keep fairly young for as long as I can. Growing older is one of my most important concerns because I have a desire to live to reach

100 years," said Lewis. He went on to say, "I often wonder what kind of a world this would be if people used the same amount of energy to help each other instead of hurting each other. That would be the answer to living in a much better world."

Greg & Helene Wurzer of Loves Park comments. "Our thoughts are about the war and we think about the billions of dollars that it is costing. Perhaps we should be spending some of those dollars to feed and clothe the poor children and mothers who are starving in those countries such as in Iraq and North Korea instead," said Helene Wurzer. "Our United Nations should be stronger in supporting the nations for the destruction of weapons of mass destruction," said Greg Wurzer.

Kenny Seay, Qtr. Master for the Loves Park VFW, Post #9759 and has been serving in this position for the past three years, was next contacted. He is a Vietnam Veteran, resides in Loves Park and has been employed with Invensys for the past 38 years. He has a grown son and daughter and is a grandfather.

"My number one issue is the economy and I worry about it for both my son and daughter. Our job market now is tough and keeping a job is somewhat difficult. However, our economy revolves around the threat of our country's coming war. I believe our economy and the war are connected. It certainly is a tough time for everyone now," said Seay

Barbara & Howard Bannen of Preservation Pointe Condominiums of Loves Park were talked with next. "Terrorists attacking and not knowing where or when it could happen. The war and the terrorists seem to be one of the same issues. They are evil and do not care about human lives. Our country has never been faced with such dreadful problems before and it is frightening. However, another important concern we have is the high cost of prescription drugs. We are hoping that Congress can get that issue on the table and pass something suitable for all the persons experiencing the rising costs of staying healthy without hardship," said Bannen.

Paul Baker of Preservation Pointe Condominiums of Loves Park comments were "No dividends because the interest rates are so low, which means seniors are living on a lot less money. Everything we buy is going up. Gasoline prices today were $1.69 per gallon. If the Harlem School Issue is passed, we will be taxed more on our property taxes to support the rising costs of our City of Loves Park," said Baker.

Granddaughter, Lynn O'Neill of Machesney Park walks and shops the mall with her Grandmother, Lorraine Shuga from New Milford each week. Lorraine Shuga resides in her home and worries about her serious arthritis condition, and takes a lot of medication for it. She has been a widow for nearly nine years after 60 years of marriage. She maintains her own home and still drives. She is the mother of 10 children and stated a wonderful life.

"I do not want to see another world war because I have lived through too many wars already. I have two grandsons in the Navy and I constantly worry about what our future holds. Our entire Church all pray for World Peace", said Shuga.

This next story was not written for the Post Journal newspaper. It was written for my mall-walking friend, Jerry Green's 90th year mother's birthday. This summer I was pleased to meet Ella and now residing in a nursing home.

ELLA'S 90TH BIRTHDAY
Written by Millie Chandler
[Editor's note: The following story appears in its original, published version]

Ella Murray was born on December 23, 1912 in Cuba City, WI. She lived there until she married Howard Birkett on November 28, 1933, at age 21. Their plans were to marry at the World's Fair in Chicago, but then decided it would be better is they married in Cuba City so family and friends could attend.

Birkett was a young farmer working on his Dad's farm in Benton, WI. They lived with his parents for a number of years while farming.

June was the first-born, followed by Jerry and both were home births. Judy was born at Doctor Terry's Hospital in Cuba. Shortly after Judy was born, they stopped farming and moved to Benton and purchased a home. Grandpa Birkett lived with them because Grandma had passed away.

Howard was a welder. Ella always told her girls, "Your Dad and his brother built the air compressor that was used to drill through rock for the construction of the highway near Dubuque, Iowa, and he built a large welding machine."

A few years later Birkett was suffering from migraine headaches and was hospitalized. Shortly after, on April 19, 1944, he died of a cerebral hemorrhage. At age 32, Ella became a widow with three young daughters to raise. It was necessary for her to work to support her young family. She did this by doing numerous jobs including house cleaning, waitress work, and head cook at school lunches. Later she worked at the Attwood Company in Stockton, IL. She always managed to provide for her family. Her daughters appreciated their mother having this ability to make them feel safe, loved and cared for.

A number of years later, Ella renewed a friendship with Melvin Peart, a widower. On September 26, 1964, Mel and Ella were married in Hazel

Green, WI and resided in a mobile home. Mel was the father of a grown son and daughter, Joe and Marsha. The girls now had a brother and Marsha had three sisters. Everyone enjoyed the well-rounded extended family. Ella's daughters loved having Mel all those years for their Dad and Joe and Marsha loved Ella.

On August 1, 1989, just lacking approximately two months of being married for 25 years, Melvin died of heart problems. Ella became a widow for the second time in her life.

All the children were grown and had their families. They all kept in close contact with Ella because she was their inspiration and they always respected their mother's love. Mother Ella was always helping or taking care of someone.

Ella continues to maintain her youthful attitude of life by being involved with all her family and friends.

She kept extremely active and had a long time devoted friendship with her friend, Elsie for many years. They walked three miles each day together when weather permitted. They were jokingly named "The Benton Street Walkers." They shared many times and hours and remained neighbors and dear friends.

Ella remains active with life and has numerous friends that constantly keep in touch with visiting and telling old family stories to each other. Ella loves to keep up with being fashionable with a desire to dress stylish. She takes care of her own home and is the proud grandmother of 18 grand-children, 36 great grandchildren, and 5 great, great grandchildren with two more on the way.

On December 23, 2002, Ella will become 90 years of age. Her birthday party will be at St. Patrick's Church Hall in Benton, Wisconsin on November 30, 2002 from 12:00 P.M to 4:00 P.M. to celebrate this wonderful birthday with all her family and friends.

"To Mom on your special day, we wish you love, good health and happiness. You have always been there for us whenever we needed anything. Today, we hope in some small way, you are loved and appreciated. Sit back, relax and enjoy your party. Today you are QUEEN FOR A DAY'. Thanks for loving us and being our mother."

/s/ June, Jerry, Judy and Marsha

... ...

The following story has a special meaning to me because I started mall walking with the drum-mer of a band, named Bun E. Carlos. I had no idea how famous this band was until several of my friends, family and others told me. Before I even knew he was a member of this rock band, we walked and talked and he told me he was with a band.

I decided it would be interesting to write a news story about being in a band. He told me this band has been traveling all over the world and Japan loves their 'Rock band'. Carlos showed me an old 78 record that was made with his group that happened to be in the Collectable Plus Store at Machesney Park Mall.

CHEAP TRICK BAND'S STORY

By Millie Chandler, For the Journal
February 2003
[Editor's note: The following story appears in its original, published version]

In an exclusive interview, Cheap Trick, the hit band from Rockford, has announced that its newest album will be released in stores around the world in April. The artwork for the CD is still in progress. More information will be available about the album later on.

Here's why you should care about Cheap Trick

Bun E. Carlos Rick Nielson Tom Petersson Robin Zander

We want you to want them

A lot will be happening before Cheap Trick's newest CD is released. The band will be meeting sometime next week in Kansas City. They will practice together for a few days before their next performance at a concert in a casino there. After that show, they have an approximate 15-city tour for the month of February. The band travels by both air and bus with a crew of seven members.

In March they will be performing in Europe in five different countries, including, Denmark, Germany, Belgium, and Holland. The last show will be performed at the Royal Albert Hall in London.

Cheap Trick has approximately 45 Gold and Platinum records in this country as well as around the world. Their music has sold approximately 16 million albums so far. They will be celebrating 30 years as a band, recording under the label of Cheap Trick, Unlimited.

"Our music is enjoyed by all age groups, including teens to some of the seniors," said band member Bun E. Carlos.

That's not bad for four guys who grew up in the Rockford area before forming their band 30 years ago.

Robin Zander graduated from Harlem High School in 1971. He is their singer and plays the guitar. He now resides in Tampa, FL with his family. The rest of the band all graduated from Guilford High School. Rick Nielsen, the lead guitar player, graduated in 1967 and resides in the Rockford area with his family. Tom Petersson, the base guitar player, graduated in 1968 and now resides in upstate New York. He will soon be moving to Nashville, TN with his family. Carlos, the band's drummer, graduated in 1969 and resides in the Rockford area with his family.

The four performed in different bands during their high school years kept running into each other at various local bands. In 1973 they formed their own band holding their practice sessions in Rick Nielsen's garage. They decided to name their new band Cheap Trick.

Their first album was released in 1976. In 1978, they had their first hit record in Tokyo, Japan. In 1979, they had their first 'Hit—Single' called "I Want You to Want Me" and that was released in the United States. In 2002, Diet Coke used it in a commercial. Part of that commercial featured a gal stating, "That was the greatest song that was ever written."

This band is extremely popular in Tokyo and has performed there many times. For the past five years, Tommy Hilfiger Company furnishes them with their performance attire and Cheap Trick band endorses the Tommy Hilfiger clothing line.

In 1997, the Cheap Trick performed and recorded their 25th Anniversary Show in down town Rockford. The concert at Davis Park drew an audience of over 10,000 persons. The band released their Silver Anniversary Recording on DVD and CD.

Band members do more than perform. Nielsen and Carlos were the honorary co-chairmen for 2002. They did the public service announcements daily during the Christmas shopping season on Channel 23 and other TV stations.

They both performed for the Mill Organization, a children's home annual benefit dinner in Rockford and entertained with 'Cheap Trick' songs to raise funds for them. Nielsen and Carlos also do some artwork, making Valentines from Artists, Writers, and collections for the Rockford College Art Gallery.

… … … …

And Here is The Rest of the Story

Sherry, my daughter in law, bought two tickets for us to attend the Cheap Trick Concert at the Coronado Theatre on Friday, April

Zander, Me & Sherry Chandler

11th, 2003 at 8:00pm in Rockford, IL. The 2500 seat theatre was sold to capacity and our balcony seats cost her $35.00 for each of us. Before attending this concert, I had walked with Carlos and asked about back stage passes. He said, he would have them for me at the ticket office, to be picked up after 6:00 pm, after stating my name. Sure enough, he had four passes for back stage, which was great.

Mike Humpal, the bike racer, told me that he was attending that concert too, because Cheap Trick was his favorite band and he would have a friend along. I said, "Watch for me and I will watch for you so we can say hello." I saw him as he was walking up the balcony. He introduced us to his friend, Russell Aldrich. I asked Humpal if he would

Aldrich & Humpal

like two back-stage passes for after the performance and he was extremely pleased. Those two guys bought long sleeve 'Cheap Trick' shirts and were delighted, because they got all four of the band members to sign their shirts.

At the concert, the band played the fan's favorite song, "I Want You to Want Me". Everyone roared, got up from their seats and sang and

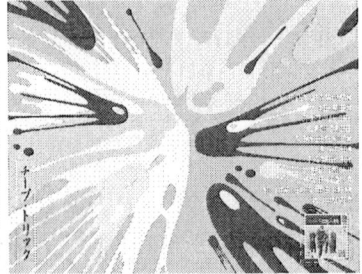

danced in place, even me.

I told my son, Jim that I was attending this concert with Sherry. Jim asked me to buy him a Cheap Trick CD. I bought their Silver Anniversary CD and at the backstage event, Bun E signed it "To

Millie, Your walking buddy, Bun E. Carlos." Besides
the signed CD, I received a hug from Bun E.,
which put a big smile on my face. There were over
one hundred people invited to attend the back
stage event. Sherry was pleased when Robin
Zander gave her a kiss on the cheek. We both had
a fantastic time.

On July 1, 2003, I was mall walking with Lou
Walker from Loves Park and somehow the conver-
sation switched to the story that was published
(see above) about the Cheap Trick Band in the
Post Journal. She told me her daughter, Cindy
Hulett, now a resident of Higginsville, Missouri
attended high School in the same class as Robin
Zander in 1971 and related this story:
During the Harlem High School Christmas
Concert, Robin Zander had a solo part in this con-
cert and he sang "Oh Holy Night". Lou Walker said,
"His voice sang out with such beauty, that he
received a standing ovation from the audience."
This memory of Walker's seemed to come to life,
as we continued walking.
Recently, I was along with my daughter-in-law,
Sherry and grandchildren, Dakota and Matthew for
some shopping. Dakota and Matthew wanted to
stop at Petco to see all the interesting pets. We
watched the poodles being trimmed and looked at
many other pets.
I happened to talk with a gal from the Rockford

area named <u>Stacy Beuster,</u> who just had her puppy groomed. I asked her what kind of a puppy he was and she told me it was a 'Yorkshire'. He was five months old. I also asked if he liked to be groomed and she told me he did. I asked what her puppy's name was and she told me it was '<u>Zander</u>', named after Robin Zander, the singer in Cheap Trick Band.

Robin Zander with guitar

Cheap Trick performed during the half-time show of Saturday's NFL game between the Tampa Bay Buccaneers and New York Jets at the Tokyo Dome in Japan. The game aired on ESPN.

On August 8th, 2003, I walked the mall with Bun E., and he told me they just returned from Tokyo, where they performed to audiences of approximately 40,000 people.

The Cheap Trick Band also had a short appearance in the movie, <u>Daddy's</u> <u>Day Care</u>.

On August 31st, 2003, Cheap Trick performed 'On the Waterfront' in Rockford following their two special guest bands, 'Harmony Riley'

Rick Nielsen & Tom Peterson

and 'The Snaggs'. They also released their new CD, "Special One," which had many great reviews.

Bun E. may be the drummer of Cheap Trick, but to me, he is my mall-walking friend.

Bun E. Carlos with drums

History & Politics in my own words
[Editor's Note: The following section appears in its original, unedited version]

Today is November 6, 2002 and elections are over. It was a long night and long past my bedtime at 2:00 am, I shut the TV off and went to sleep.

Some of the tightest races were in Minnesota. One week before Election Day, Paul Wellstone, his wife Sheila, one of their daughters and two pilots were killed in an airplane crash while flying to a funeral. Two minutes before they reached the runway, something went wrong. Their pilot made a turn away from the airport, they crashed and were killed. What a tragedy it was for their family, the MN Senate, their friends, and our country?

Minnesota is a heavily populated Democratic state and Wellstone was returning for his third term in office, even though he said, he would be a two-term Senator. Very quickly, the Democratic Party had a major problem and decided the best Democrat they could replace Wellstone with was former Vice-President, Walter Mondale. He agreed to serve his party.

The memorial for Wellstone turned into a Political Rally instead of a memorial service. Senator Trent Lott attended this service as did many other political persons, and was booed.

President Clinton, Senator Clinton and Tom Daschle were also there among thousands of others. Jessie Ventura got disgusted with the political display of events and walked out. This turned off many persons that were supposed to be at a memorial service.

Norman Coleman was planning his campaign against Paul Wellstone and now the game plan changed. Walter Mondale was his new running mate for the last five days of the campaign. A one-hour debate was scheduled between Mondale and Coleman. Mondale is a brilliant politician but he looked old and tired at 74 and his ideas seemed old and tired as well. Coleman pulled this race off with a 50% lead over Mondale with a 48% following.

I always liked Norm Coleman when I lived in Minnesota and voted for him for Governor, but Jessie Ventura became the new Governor. Ventura became very rich while he was serving as governor, not from his salary, but from all the sidelines he had because he was the governor. He had 'Jessie Dolls', 'Jessie shirts' and was on National media many times because he was good coverage. You never knew what he was going to say and the media loved Jessie. He was always making the news. He wrote books and managed to be a referee at a wrestling match, while being Governor.

My friend, Mike was a devout Democrat and I

was on the other side. At the MN State Fair when all the politicians were shaking hands with their constituents, I wanted to visit my favorite Senator, Rudy Buschowich. My friend wanted me to visit his favorite Senator Wellstone, so we made a deal.

He would stand in line with me and I would stand in line with him. I have heard Wellstone, many times. I decided to ask this question. "I am a Republican. Could you give me a good reason why my vote should be for you?" I do not remember his answer.

My friend, Mike knew the Wellstones well and he wanted me to meet, Sheila and introduced me to her saying, "I would like you to meet my friend, Sheila." I shook hands with her, but decided to ask her the same question. "Why should I vote for Paul?" She took both of my hands into her hands and said, "Millie, Paul is my husband and I love him very much and that is why I think you should vote for Paul." I thought that was the greatest answer I could have ever received and have never forgotten it.

My friend, Mary Newman from Edina, MN, told me in a letter, "I think something was very wrong with that crash because they were two miles out from the airport." Sure enough, she was right.

On November 10, 2002, the Sunday Star Tribune newspaper of the Twin Cities had a front-page story written by Tony Kennedy and Paul McEnroe, Star Tribune Staff writers and here are parts of that story. "The pilot-in-command of the plane that carried Sen. Paul Wellstone to his death exaggerated his flying experience by telling managers at Executive Aviation he had 400 to 500 hours of prime experience at a major commuter airline, American Eagle."

"Corney, the pilot only trained there. He never was named a first officer or co-plot at the airline and never flew a passenger flight at American Eagle," the official said. "In fact, Corney was sentenced to Federal Prison on fraud charges a week after he resigned from American Eagle. Cory was a licensed pilot and had flown private planes over the years. But at American Eagle, "He never carried passengers," the official said. "He never flew a scheduled flight." That is the real story of why Wellstone and his family and everyone crashed on that devastating event in personal and political history.

Another Senate race, I was interested in was the one for Elizabeth Dole. I liked her. On July 19, 1998, I was taking a class in Counseling Theories and Techniques. For a class project I wrote a special paper and called it "What everyone might want to know, but never asked or could be called, "Whatever."

I gave my presentation in front of the class for a final project. The information came from Lillian Glass, PhD's book <u>Attracting Terrific People</u>. Over a hundred people, including men and women, between the ages of 16 and 67 were asked "What was the first thing that attracted them to another person?" The top three answers were the eyes, the body, and the smile. In this survey, no one mentioned the voice or the way a person spoke, even though research shows us that the way a person speaks has an incredibly powerful impact on how we feel about him or her and how we relate to that person.

I further wrote about, Kate White's <u>Secrets of Women Who Get</u> <u>Everything They Want</u> "I'm advising you a sweet-talker; no matter how much it runs against the grain, the strategy used by women, usually get what they want. I finally recognized the truth that day, you really can catch more flies with honey than with vinegar. That day everyone was having a terrible time getting seats on a plane and Elizabeth Dole was among them." This was a few years before our disaster of 9.11.

Suddenly the publisher opened her mouth and in the most honeyed voice said something like, "Harry (she read his name tag), we are so exhausted from our trip and we can't even think straight. We desperately need your help. What would you suggest is the best thing for us to do?" I believe we got bumped up to first class. It was like magic. I finally recognized the truth that day. Since that plane ride I've had a heightened sensitivity to this art, and I've paid attention to the women who are masters at it. The woman who apparently wrote the book on it is Elizabeth Dole.

She was the keynote speaker at a "Redbook" luncheon in Washington and was unbelievably charismatic and dynamic and personable. Dole asked people about themselves, hung on their every word, and never appeared bored with what any one was saying. She is masterful at getting her way. I believe Elizabeth Dole will be a terrific Senator for NC.

Prior to the last few days of campaigning for the 2002 election, President Bush traveled to 10 or 11 states in the last two days of campaigning and giving his support to the delegates. He was called a marathon President running the most supportive dynamic race of his life. Every place he stopped, he was welcomed with a roar of approval at the political party's gatherings.

Iraqi Freedom as Private Citizen
[Editor's Note: The following section appears in its original, unedited version]

On March 16th, 2003, I wrote in my journal, Sunday night, 10:00 PM. I think we will be in a war within two or three days. Saddam said, "If we go to war with Iraq, he will have us attacked on land, sea or air, anywhere or place in the entire world." And then I closed my journal for that night.

On March 17th, I wrote at 9:30 PM, "We are now on 'High Alert', the orange level. President Bush just presented his final plan to Saddam Hussein giving 48 hours for him and his sons to leave Iraq or be held responsible for the past 12 years of lies and danger he is causing his own people and the entire world."

On March 18th, it was stated that all our Armed Forces in Kuwait were probably saying and thinking, "Hurry up and Wait" and "It's time to go."

On March 19, 2003, at 9:15 PM, Central Time, in a 10-minute speech, our President made an official address to the American People and said, "We are now officially at War."

Tony Blair was the United States strongest supporter in this war. The United Kingdom Armed Forces fought this war along with our military forces. There were a number of other countries supporting us as well.

This war was not popular with many persons, both in our country as well as around the world. There were many strong and determined protestors demonstrating and coming together to support their views against this war.

Our American freedoms must not be attacked by terrorism and it is an unfortunate situation that we were not prepared for the attack on our country with the 9.11 Trade Towers being destroyed and the Pentagon. If the terrorists had their way, they would have attacked our White House, as well.

A terrorist who becomes a 'human bomber' where their officials pay their families thousands of dollars to commit these terrorist acts in the name of their religion will no longer be tolerated from democracies throughout the world.

Terrorism is the most difficult and costly challenge we will ever endure. Perhaps, they feel their cause will be benefited because they are destroying our valued freedoms and democracies that are so precious to us.

Wars are not something we want to happen and too many lives are lost. Even one single life lost is one too many when Americans and other free nations value freedom as their most precious thing they have. It must be protected and fought for at any cost.

There are many countries in our world that does not have the opportunity of being free. Women in many countries are not free to do the things their male populations are allowed.

It is amazing to be able to sit in our living rooms and watch the war take place before our eyes. It makes a person wonder how fast and far our world of technology has moved our lives to bring us all world events as soon as they happen. We are no longer a democracy spaced far away by oceans and continents and have become a smaller world because of technology. It becomes a major concern and problems when one country produces nuclear weapons that could destroy other countries.

The hospital that our troops put up in a few days in Kuwait was astonishing. It was put up in huge tents and had all the surgery equipment that would be necessary for most procedures. They had four or more medical doctors that have put their civilian life on hold to come aboard with their reservist units and serve. They had many skilled nurses to assist and treat patients that were not in as great danger. Many beds were installed in this hospital unit. There wasn't air-conditioning in this hospital and it was not comfortable as a regular hospital. The doctors and nurses' worked around the clock and military wounds were top priority.

The top news journalists were embedded with the troops bringing the world up to date, 'minute by minute' of what was going on. I particularly enjoyed watching David Bloom riding on the front tank with the 3rd Marine Unit. He had rigged up this tank so he could broadcast these reports as he traveled through the deserts, through sandstorms and battles. I watched him day by day and I started getting concerned because he looked like he was getting too much sun and wind blowing at him and his hair started to become unruly and he took on the rugged look of being tired.

He always gave his photographer credit by

broadcasting, I want my photographer, (and he would call him by name), to get this shot. Bloom became part of the crew and associated with many of the service persons in the unit. He even called his wife, had her get one of the men's wives that just had a new child, at her phone so she could talk with her husband.

David Bloom's communication to the world was alive with spirit and determination of how they were proceeding through the sand storms and how long it took for the men to fix one of their tanks, only to have it blow up again. He made the war real and seemed to bring us all along with them. It was exciting to see him and his 'Bloom-mobile' because of his enthusiastic journalist reporting with his enormous motivation.

I felt like he was part of my family. The sadness that I experienced with his death was deep. It made me want to grieve with all his fellow journalists, his marine unit, and last but not least with his beautiful wife and three lovely daughters he always talked about. He loved his family with all his heart. It was a sad day for our country and the world. He was a great journalist that loved doing this last assignment and the world will always remember David Bloom as a hero that died before his time at age 39.

The third division of the Marine Tank Unit all felt a huge void with the death of David Bloom as they have all come to know him and formed a true bond with this energetic embedded journalist. They held their own special funeral service for David Bloom and this unit suffered a great loss just as if they lost one of their own marines.

The NBC Journalists all had many stories to tell of David Bloom and how excited he had been about this assignment. Tom Brokaw said, "He stopped by my office about three times in one day to ask various questions about many things. He wanted to be a great journalist and he was." All his viewing audiences will miss him. Most of all, his wife, three young daughters and all his family and friends.

Jessica Lynch was one of the success stories of this war. This young pretty 19-year-old soldier enlisted into military service so she would have the opportunity to get her college education paid for. She was a lovely gal that wanted to become a teacher. Her unit took a wrong turn on the desert road and ran into an ambush. They were attacked and she was among the ones taken prisoners of war.

Her family was on TV a number of times and her father did most of the talking in his very quiet and sad manner. The family was extremely worried and afraid for their daughter and what will become of her. The joyous part of this war was when the rescue of Jessica Lynch took place.

An Iraqi citizen knew where this female prisoner was being held and he risked his life by going to the U.S. Armed Forces and reported this information. He even drew a map showing exactly where this American girl was taken. She had been shot and was in serious condition.

The military arranged a secret mission and with precision movements, they found her and one of the men said to her, "I'm an American soldier and don't be afraid." She took his hand and said, "I'm a soldier too, and please don't leave me."

What a joyous time it was for the world to have this brave soldier saved and it made me feel proud to see that one American is very important to all Americans. This young courageous soldier had been shot in both legs and her arm. She had a lot of healing and surgery performed to get her on the road to recovery.

Her family was delighted and again, her father and mother were on National TV. Everyone in our country, her community of family and friends and all the troops serving in Iraq were feeling the joy. Jessica Lynch was alive and she became our American hero. She has been awarded a full scholarship. It was a great day to see her return from our hospital in Germany, together with her family. They were flown over to be with her in the hospital there. Jessica will undergo more surgeries in the military hospitals in the United States.

Looting was a major issue. Everyone was helping them selves to whatever they could carry away. I was delighted to see this Iraqi woman carry out approximately eight large heavy type dinner plates that she looted from one of the castles. I thought to myself, "She deserves those treasured china plates as a reward for all the suffering under Saddam's dictatorship of many years."

Another thing that impressed me was seeing another young lady that had her young son, wheeling on a caster, a filing cabinet that came from one of the castles. Again, I thought that was an appropriate piece of merchandise, she deserved. I loved seeing that little boy beat up on the head of Saddam's broken statute that finally came down with our assistance.

The corporal on the top of the military jeep teaching all the little boys how to sing a song putting smiles on their faces. It was about time the young children had someone encouraging them it is okay to smile, sing, and have fun. I thought how wonderful it was for this soldier to bring so much joy to these little children, having them singing and happy for a few minutes of their lives. It was played over and over again. This young corporal was interviewed and some of the media said he should be our 'Public Relations' person to bring peace to the Iraqi people.

It delighted me to see the first huge poster of Saddam being torn down and a lot of joy coming to the Iraqi people and then some Iraqis were giving our troops flowers because of their happiness showing everyone, at last the Americans were here to help them.

It was another victory when the POW's were rescued and were brought home. We still have military missing in action and I hope more will have happy endings. Iraq continues to be full of terrorism and constant danger. Americans are proud of our great military working on this major difficult mission.

On August 1, 2003, <u>Stone Phillips on NBC, Date Line</u>, had a special program on the Story of Unit 507 called <u>Ambush</u>. <u>Shoshana Johnson</u> was one of the members along with Jessica and the others that took the wrong turn in the road. Shoshana was a cook for the military, but serving in combat duty. She felt heart break and was scared. The sand was awful and speed was important. This unit fell behind and missed a turn. The route was not clear causing them to drive into a disaster and they came under fire. She had no idea that Jessica Lynch was alive.

Their Code of Conduct was that you resist until you no longer can. She thought all the prisoners were taken hostage and probably all killed. The wonderful Marines found Shawna as she remembered that they kicked down the door and said, "We're taking you home."

At Fort Bliss, TX, the returned prisoners of war were honored and it was a 'big deal'. Our country was proud.

Today was a big day – July 22, 2003

[Editor's Note: The following section appears in its
original, unedited version]

This morning I happened to be watching the 'Today Show' before I left for my daily four-mile walk at Machesney Park Mall. They were going to interview Senator Bob Dole and Senator Elizabeth Dole together because it was Senator Bob Dole's 80th birthday today. I could not help being extremely interested in this interview. He looked spectacular, as did Senator, Elizabeth Dole. It brought back memories for me because on October 23, 1996, I was enrolled in Political Science 101 at NHCC in Brooklyn Park, MN and I wrote a paper for 'Candidates in the 1996 Elections.' The title was – '1996 Election of Values'

My first paragraph said, "President Bill Clinton and Bob Dole and our entire country faces one of the greatest challenges for the 1996 elections and in one word can be described as the election of values.

President Clinton was re-elected and Bob Dole retired. However, he remains involved with many political challenges and has been working with both parties on special projects. "Happy Birthday Bob Dole."

Jessica Lynch was coming home and there were great events planned in Elizabeth, West Virginia for this 'Home Coming'. However, some breaking news was also happening concerning 'Iraqi Freedom'.

One of our greatest successes of this Iraqi war happed today. After a six-hour gun battle, our Special Armed Forces succeeded in shooting down and killing, Uday and Qusay, Saddam Hussein's most feared sons. They were responsible for brutally murdering millions of innocent Iraqis.

Unfinished business is to find Saddam Hussein, Dictator of over three decades and bring him to justice, whether it is 'dead or alive' and our continuing mission is to find 'Weapons of Mass Destruction'. Each day we hope will bring us closer to restoring a better, safer and more normal life to the Iraqi people.

The returning of Jessica Lynch to her home community was terrific. She looked great and gave her first public appearance to the world. Her brother, Greg, also a soldier in uniform, introduced Jessica in military uniform. What a joy it was for everyone.

Lynch expressed her gratitude to the many persons that were involved in her capture. She went on to say she was grateful that most of her unit was freed from being 'Prisoners of War'. Lynch went on to express her sorrow for her best friend that was killed in that battle and said, "She will always be remembered in my heart." She also went on to thank the doctors and everyone who participated in her recovery. She still has more recovery to undergo, but the doctors feel she will recover 100%.

Jessica told everyone, she remembered when she was captured. Someone said, "I am an American Soldier." While they were carrying her on a stretcher, she replied, "I am an American Soldier, too."

The sign in the front of the <u>New Hope Baptist Church in Palestine</u> where the Lynch family attends had posted, "God is still in the business of making miracles and one of the miracles has come home today."

Lynch received the 'Purple Heart', the 'P.O.W. Metal', and the 'Bronze Star' for combat. Jessica Lynch, today, represented every member of the Armed Forces, making us all proud to be Americans.

(On December 14, 2003 – "We got him." Saddam Husseim was caught alive, the Ace of Spades in the deck of cards, was brought out of a 'Spider Hole' looking like a homeless bum. We are just one step closer to 'Iraqi Freedom'.)

Fifty Years Ago Today -July 27, 2003
Korean Reunion of our Veterans

Today, many Korean Veterans met in South Korea to celebrate a troop reunion. In 1953, they were young men and woman, serving our country in that war. Many were killed, never to return to their families and loved ones again. Taps were play at the conclusion of their 50th reunion honoring all the troops who died.

The Aging Process

Yes, that's where we are all heading. It is called 'Life'. We hope to age with grace, charm and dignity. That's the way it is suppose to go. But is that the way I want it to happen? My answer is "Heck, No". "I will fight the 'aging process' every bit of the way, because who wants to grow older? Not me."

It's not a choice. It happens. Some morning while getting out of bed, our bones and muscles may ache with pain and we wonder why. After all, seventy-six is not old. There may be many more things you have on your plate. There are things to do, read, learn, be involved with every day and watch our grandchildren grow up. We need more time.

Questions we ask may be "Where did I leave my keys? What did I come into the bedroom to get? What is that person's name? I just met her or him the other day? Why can't I remember something that seemed to be important?

Medications become a major part of our lives. Exercising and eating properly are top priorities. But why do the added pounds and inches seem to be coming out of nowhere and attaching to our bodies, requiring us to purchase larger sizes? The bottom line is this: We are in charge of our own bodies and that is the most important reason to take care of ourselves.

Time is precious and everyday the 'sun shines' is a good day. A smile from someone, a kind word, a friendly hello and a 'how are you' are all important. In today's society, we look around and the communities seem to be growing older.

When attending Metropolitan State University, I took every class in Gerontology that was available. Yes, I was the oldest student in every class. I did not feel old and continued to think all the training was about someone older than me.

The amount of knowledge and living we have chalked up in our lives are valuable and memorable for our families. We can share these yesterdays with them while we take one-step each day into our tomorrows.

Now, I find, "Yes, Millie, you are included in what

the study of gerontology is. Yes, Millie, you are facing the 'Aging Process' whether you like it or not." "All you learned in college applies to you and everyone in our continuously, growing older society." Accepting the aging process has finally become a reality for me. Another page in my life has been turned.

Sometime in 1999, I attended an <u>AARP</u> convention with my friend, Shirley, to research a paper I was going to write for one of my gerontology classes. This convention was a four-day event. We managed to see and do everything we wanted to do in one day. We listened to speeches given by <u>Hugh Downs, Vice-President, Al Gore</u> and <u>Louis Rukeyser</u> and enjoyed this huge convention.

The highlight of the day, as far as I was concerned, was the opportunity to have my picture taken with <u>Willard Scott</u>, then the age of seventy-one, compliments of <u>Metropolitan Life Insurance Company</u>. I did not have to wait to get my picture on Willard Scott's famous jars of

Willard Scott & Me

Smucker's 100 year - birthday celebration'.

My Friend, Mary Newman

Mary has been a close friend for over fifty years and a family friend of the Chandler family her entire life. Prior to her stroke sometime during the early part of 2003, I visited her during the Memorial Day weekend of 2002. Mary, Shirley and me had all spent the entire weekend together, visiting a lot of our relatives and friends in central Minnesota.

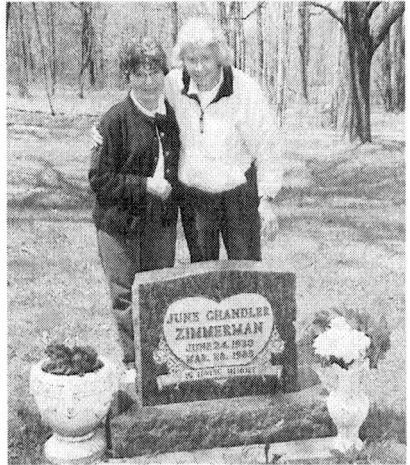

The most important visit for Mary was to place large flower arrangements on her parent's gravesites and a smaller arrangement on her lifelong friend June Zimmerman's grave. June was my also sister in law.

A stroke is a terrible thing. Mary and I had been writing to each other at least once every week. Her handwriting was beautiful while mine is extremely poor. I envied her writing, but was pleased to have my wonderful computer to write my letters. Mary can no longer write and this is only one of the things she can no longer do.

Prior to her stroke, she was extremely busy, with her job, house in the Minneapolis area and with her family and lake properties in central Minnesota. Mary also was a good 'black jack player' and enjoyed driving to the casinos fairly often. She also had two large beautiful Persian white cats.

I write to her each week and her friend, Fritz, does the physical writing for Mary, so I can still keep in touch with her. She has attempted to write with the hand that was not affected by the stroke and in time, this may be possible. Anyone's life can take many turns and changes and recovery and hope is part of the process.

Friends are one of our life's most important assets. Life is indeed precious, and every single minute of every single day, we should remember to thank the Lord for another good day.

The End of the Line

THE end OF THE line

Time seems to be running out for the once ubiquitous pay phone. The ever-increasing use of cellular phones has created a disconnect with coin calling that figures to make pay phones obsolete.

1889 – The inventor of the pay phone, William Gray, installs the first coin-operated phone in a bank in Hartford, Conn. His invention replaced public phones with attendants who collect the money.

1920 – Telephones present in about 35 percent of American households.

1983 – The first commercial cellular phone network is launched in Chicago.

2001 – With cellular phones more commonplace, BellSouth Corp. decides to give up its 143,000 pay phones.

1876 – Boston inventor Alexander Graham Bell invents the telephone.

1905 – The first outdoor pay phone is placed on a Cincinnati street. However, outdoor public phones don't become widespread until the 1950s.

1960 – The Bell System installs its millionth pay phone.

1996 – With cellular phones still frequently viewed as a luxury, the number of pay phones hits its peak at about 2.6 million.

2003 – Half of Americans have cellular phones, and 95 percent of households have phones. There are only about 1.8 million pay phones.

SOURCES: AT&T; American Public Communications Council; Federal Communications Commission   AP

269

Sometime in 2003, I read an article pertaining to the end of telephone booths. The telephone companies have been loosing money, due to the cost of maintaining them. And with cell phones, they are not used to the extent they used to be. Today, every one in the world seems to be connected with technology and the use of cell phones. The telephone booth will become a piece of our changing history.

This article seemed to have some relevance because I, too, am coming to the end of the line with my story. There were two more important subjects to write about...My two youngest grandchildren,

Dakota Chandler at age three

Dakota and Matthew Chandler, residing in Kingston, IL.

Dakota Chandler

During the past years, Dakota has asked me,

"Grandma, are we going to be in your book?" She was told, "Yes, Dakota, I think you will be."

For a few years, Dakota was into the 'American Doll' phase. She always wanted things, another doll, and clothing outfits for the doll or some of the American Girl Books. Although the 'American Girl' line is expensive, Dakota does her part to buy these items with the money she earns from helping do chores in her household.

Sherry bought Greg a 'Cappuccino machine' for Christmas a number of years ago and after Greg learned to use it, he taught Dakota how to make 'Cappuccinos'. He agreed to pay her 50 cents per cup for every cup she made. Dakota became a pro at making Cappuccinos and when Greg is driving from the airport to his home after flying, he calls Dakota on his cell phone to ask her to prepare his Cappuccino, letting her know that he will be home in the next twenty minutes, giving her plenty of time to have it ready.

Dakota is a gal that knows how to earn her own money and spend it as well. Dakota also earns money by doing most of the yard mowing. She is practically a 'pro' with the John Deere riding lawnmower. Recently, she decided that a laptop computer would be helpful for doing her schoolwork. She talked with her mom and dad and they made a deal. If Dakota saved enough to pay for one half of the laptop, her parents would pay for the other half. She did not have quite enough for her half, so she made another deal. "Instead of paying anymore money towards a laptop, I will make Dad all the cups of Cappuccino he wants from now on without charge." Dakota told me about that and said she wished she had never made that deal. Greg breaks down every now and then and pays her the 50 cents anyway.

On December 11th, 2003, Dakota turned twelve and is now taller than her Grandma. This soon to be, 'young lady' had been in the top level of all her classes in every subject.

Before Christmas of 2003, I asked Dakota what she wanted for Christmas. She hesitated slightly and with a smile in her voice said, "Money." On December 26th, she sweet-talked her mother into taking her shopping to 'Old Navy' and she used her Christmas money to buy herself the things she wanted. She told me today what she bought and said, "Grandma, I got it all for half-price."

I believe Dakota someday will be an "Entrepreneur" or a CEO of some large company. She will not only know how to spend money, but how to earn it as well. I am proud to be her Grandma.

Matthew Chandler's World

On April 20th, 2003, Sherry, Dakota and Matthew were at my home. As usual, Matthew headed for the basement, his favorite hangout. That is where the toy box is, another TV, a child's school desk and all the comforts of any playroom. In order to keep Matthew occupied and happy, I just give him plenty of paper to draw on and let him have his own space.

He loves to play, draw, watch TV, build things, read cereal boxes, loves French fries, pizza, and lots of fruits. He comes up with numerous and outstanding ideas. Matthew's vocabulary is excellent and he is polite, remembering to say 'Please' and 'Thank you'.

Sherry, recently enrolled Matthew in 'rock dancing' lessons and he loves them. "I'm going to become the 'King of Rock'," said Matthew. A few weeks ago, he had a terrific dance lesson and asked his mother, "Do you think I did good?" She said, "Yes, you did Matthew." He then said, "Do you think Elvis's soul would be proud of me?"

On this date, Matthew drew and colored a picture for me. It is filled with color and very imaginative. I requested him to sign it. Matthew loves to play with his swords and shield and imagines himself the hero. He also knows by name, every kind of dinosaur our world knows about, which is much beyond my comprehension. The next day, I had an enormous need

Mathew's Drawing

to find a proper frame for Matthew's colorful drawing.

In my kitchen, just above the cook range, the paint had begun to peel and the wall looked terrible and was in dire need of repair. I talked to my son, Greg about this emergency work that needed to be taken care of. At our next visit to the Home Depot, I picked up a sample of tile to match the area. The first choice of tile was a neutral tone of beige because that was the most reasonably priced tile.

After I put Matthew's, colorful picture on the wall, the choice of tile switched to black. It had to be black tile to match both the trims on the range and Matthew's delightful black framed drawing.

Yes, Greg has completed the professional job of tile work above my range and it looks great. He told me, "Mother, I used to have one house I had to worry about, but now I have yours, too."

Back to Matthews world…After looking at Matthew's picture of a little boy with a big sword facing an evil monster, Grandma Millie made up her own story about this picture. My story goes something like this…

Mathew's picture represented a plot like 'Spiderman's' story. 'Spiderman's' creator imagined one of the bugs he played with as a little boy becoming a hero. Spiderman helped save the world from all the bad happenings of the Great Depression of the 1930's, giving the little boy hope.

I began to see Matthew's drawing in a different prospective, and here is my story. In this picture, Matthew becomes the hero and has the big sword to keep the world safe. Perhaps, he represents every 'American' that believes in all our freedoms that we all to often take for granted. For me, the monster dinosaur became the terrible state of dangerous terrorism in the world.

I think that my grandson, Matthew, and all other children, have the opportunity to achieve whatever they choose because we have freedom. They can follow their heart and their dreams for the future.

Our children and grandchildren will inherit our

world. I hope we can leave them a peaceful land without fear of 'terrorism'. I hope and pray for better things for all of our tomorrows.

"Yes, this is the end of the line, because after more than five years of thinking about writing this book and finally deciding how I would be able to include everything important, I have finally completed this complicated challenge of the pages of life."

'Grandma Millie' is closing down the computer and turning off the lights in her office. This is the end of 'A Mother's Story of Changing Times'.

Acknowledgements

A special thanks to the many
persons that assisted me.

Darlene Yock, my neighbor, a retired teacher, the Secretary of Preservation Pointe Association, and now my friend for her diligent assistance with the preliminary editing. She said, "It is like the blind leading the blind."

My son Richard and his wife Bonnett, for the major editing and publishing of this book.

Cliff Chandler for sending me information included.

My sons James, Richard and Greg for informationrequested.

My daughter-in-law, Sherry for information requested.

Tom Bloom, my Journalist Instructor at North Hennepin Community College for giving me the opportunity to have a desire to write.

Dan Moeller, Editor of the Post Journal, a local community newspaper of Rock Valley Publishing in Machesney Park, IL.

Morrison County Record Newspaper – Mabel Sanders Story.

Copyright Rockford Register Star 2003. (Cheap Trick Photos)

GKK – Genoa – Kingston – Kirkland Weekly Newspaper (Photo)

Aqence France-Press photo – taken in honor of White House 200th Anniversary.

Associated Press – end of the line telephone booth

Tom Brokaw's, NBC Special – Traffic Controllers, (in my own words.)

Stone Phillips, Date Line - Unit 507 - Ambush – Shoshana Johnson.

Gloria Fay, Property Manager of Machesney Park Mall for the opportunity to have a "Book Signing" here.

Bun E. Carlos, Drummer for Cheap Trick Band &

members

Gloria Fay, Property Manager of Machesney Park Mall for the opportunity and necessary assistance to publish my book.

Dale R. Steinke, Radio Shack Manager, Machesney Park Mall, with scanning of all pictures.

M.K. Publishing for binding and printing this book.

The list continues and I am grateful for everyone that contributed to making A Mother's Story of Changing Times, a reality.